Over-50

Over-50
How We Keep Working

Jane Genova
Preface by Taryn Simpson

Outskirts Press, Inc.
Denver, Colorado

The opinions expressed in this manuscript are solely the opinions of the author and do not represent the opinions or thoughts of the publisher. The author has represented and warranted full ownership and/or legal right to publish all the materials in this book.

Over-50: How We Keep Working
All Rights Reserved.
Copyright © 2010 Jane Genova
v2.0

This book may not be reproduced, transmitted, or stored in whole or in part by any means, including graphic, electronic, or mechanical without the express written consent of the publisher except in the case of brief quotations embodied in critical articles and reviews.

Outskirts Press, Inc.
http://www.outskirtspress.com

ISBN: 978-1-4327-5660-4

Outskirts Press and the "OP" logo are trademarks belonging to Outskirts Press, Inc.

PRINTED IN THE UNITED STATES OF AMERICA

*Dedicated to Amy C. Karnilowicz
who got me back working in 2003*

Contents

Preface ix
Introduction xiii
Chapter 1: Black Swans: Humans plan, the gods laugh 1
Chapter 2: We Like This Job: How to hold onto it 7
Chapter 3: Finding Our Next Job, Assignment,
   Or Business Venture 13
Chapter 4: Change, Stuck, Change, Stuck 19
Chapter 5: We Got To Want To Work 29
Chapter 6: We Are Our Stories:
   Those can be liabilities or assets 35
Chapter 7: Resumes Tell Employers Stories
   They Want To Hear 45
Chapter 8: Cover Letters as Performance Art 51
Chapter 9: Interviews Are Two-Way Street 57
Chapter 10: Our Unique Power Strategies 67
Chapter 11: Adversity Is Good 75
Chapter 12: Thinking the Unthinkable: Going blue collar 83
Chapter 13: Being a Late Bloomer 89
Conclusion 95
About the Author 97

Preface

When Jane Genova had sent me her concept for coaching and conducting workshops for those over-50 in this new economy, I thought to myself: *Pure brilliance.* My first career had been in Human Resources. I myself am over-50. That means that I know the power and potential for those of us over-50, including myself.

After all, we have the decades of experience in the workplace. We bore witness to all the fads such as quality circles, the excesses like way too complex investment vehicles, and the emerging realities such as doing more with less manpower. We have survived and often thrived amidst all that.

Therefore, despite our undertow of angst, we are convinced we can plant ourselves in even rocky soil, start sprouting buds, and eventually bloom. A growing number of us are distinct late bloomers like Hillary Clinton, Clint Eastwood, Pema Chordon, and David Letterman. Incidentally, University of Chicago economics researcher David W. Galenson confirms there is such a phenomenon.

We over-50 can and likely will create new markets, new jobs, new models for the workplace. In this protean economy, we are the capitalist version of John Adams and Thomas Jefferson.

OVER-50: HOW WE KEEP WORKING

This, not the birth of democracy, may be the biggest experiment Americans will live through and likely designate a national holiday to celebrate.

A few years later, Jane Genova then told me that those over-50 wanted her to publish a book on the topic. She asked me to write the Preface. I was: *Beyond Honored*. Now I had joined the other Stay-Working Fighters on the front lines.

Here is what I see happening. The economic uncertainty and volatility had initially thrown some of us, but not for long. As we embrace this as The New Normal we recognize that whether we want to be stars or simply keep working, we have to approach and do work differently. That concept of working for The Man for 40 years and retiring on a cushy pension and health benefits in addition to Social Security all are by now an Aesop's Fable. That concept lies along with the dinosaur remains collecting dust in the Smithsonian. Then there is the mantra of four or five generations working side-by-side for the first time in human history. All I can say is, not for long, my friend.

The workplace is changing faster than anyone would have guessed. As a former Human Resources leader turned ghostwriter and novelist, I hold firm in my forecasting that large corporations are a thing of the past. Gone are the days of becoming and staying an "employee." While companies may hire a few key employees, the vast majority will be consultants. There will be no "The Man," only peers pulling together to solve problems, cost-efficiently. No more health benefits, no more retirement benefits, no more employee AND employer taxes. To each his own, mono a mono.

Having made those bold statements, I am convinced that the generation best equipped to handle this dramatic change in corporate

PREFACE

America are the Baby Boomers. We did, after all, learn how to operate computers on the job. We created the idea of "overtime." We thrived on burning the candle at both ends. And we greeted the new millennium first hand.

We are the generation of change. It only makes sense that the generation who has seen technology take on a life of its own becomes the example of learning how to work after the age of 50. I promise you will refer to this book time and time again to capture every pearl of wisdom. In this day and age, it only makes sense to experience transformation in your career. That piece of common career sense comes from a musician turned accountant, turned Human Resources expert, turned Information Technology consultant, turned ghostwriter/novelist, turned video consultant/creator. Regarding the latter, here is the video trailer I created for Jane Genova's novel "The Fat Guy From Greenwich" http://www.youtube.com/watch?v=tIWY1o2Efxk.

~Taryn Simpson
Pulitzer Prize Competitor for "The Mango Tree Café, Loi Kroh Road"
Http://author-tarynsimpson.blogspot.com
Www.twitter.com/writer4762

Introduction

We over-50 represent nearly a third of the U.S. workforce [Source: U.S. Chamber of Commerce.] Most of us want to and/or need to keep it just that way, that is, employed at a job or self-employed. Currently, there are a growing number of versions of being employed.

We work 80 hours a week as partners in a law firm. Those 80 hours include dinners with prospects as we develop new business.

We are Chief Executive Officers of the Fortune 500.

We are self-employed.

We have been at the same part-time job at a major corporation for 20 years.

We are free agents employed just-in-time by temporary agencies. Some of our bookings last 18 months or more.

We are embedded in underground economies, walking dogs, running errands, transporting those who cannot drive to the casino.

OVER-50: HOW WE KEEP WORKING

We are novelists, psychics, and actors.

Likely, we will not be doing what we are doing now until we decide to stop working. We sense that. Already change in our employment status may have come unexpectedly and grabbed us by the throat. We promise ourselves and our families: *That will not happen again.* But change, usually unanticipated, will. Again and again and again. And we will bounce back from that and find another way to make a living or to prevent our needing to dig into our retirement funds. That is the way it has played out, for many of us who have been rocked by career shocks, large and small.

That is what this book is about: Keeping us working, no matter what. Even if the U.S. economy stabilizes and begins to grow in a consistent manner, our world of work will remain a rollercoaster. Companies will fold, outsource, downsize, switch strategic focus. Customers will develop new tastes, values, and price points. Clients will die, retire, get fired, merge, or adapt technologies we do not excel in. We will discover we are bottom-fishing in our familiar niche business.

Some of that rollercoaster ride will land us on top. Our talent in delivering motivational speeches catapults us into the big time. We earn $30,000 a speech. Our client's software is purchased by a Fortune 100 company and we are needed to tell that story in press releases, tweets, videos for YouTube, and white papers. We receive a promotion to become the Chief Executive Officer, after being a shrewd number-two who stayed in the background for years. Our new niche in advising the Y Generation on investing grows so quickly we have to hire other financial consultants. We are considering if we should create a franchise.

That means there is no returning to settling in. Not for us. Not

INTRODUCTION

now. Not ever. Getting too comfortable will not be in the cards, not ever again.

There had been that Ford Motor slogan in the mid 1990s. It was: Quality is job number-one. For us over-50, keeping working is job number-one. Not that it is all that difficult. Actually I have come to relish the strategic and tactical chase after work.

What is tough is that it is not what we over-50 had become used to. Up until the past several years, our career paths, ranging from journalism and law to plumbing and construction, have been linear, predictable, and set up for us to consume. There the jobs were, sitting right there on the shelf. We took the job we wanted and consumed it as the good Americans we were. Our conditioning had been to belly up to the economy and take what we wanted, including a job, career path, or even shot at self employment.

If one industry or company disappeared, there were ready-made formulas to head in another direction. They included degree programs, certificate training, gaining experience under the radar in an ally's office, and going to work in our brother-in-law's business. As the MAD MAGAZINE mascot Alfred E. Newman used to say: *What me worry.* Not much and not for long.

No longer is that the situation. Increasingly we are discovering that we have to produce our careers, often from bits and pieces of raw material. They are not on the shelf in any career shop.

When there were still prestigious freelance journalism assignments to be had, Laurel Touby tried some of them out in media capital Manhattan. No fool, she sensed that was not going to be a lucrative way to establish herself. She looked at her strengths. From the South, she had a grace and charm which pulled people toward her. That led to hosting casual media parties. During those get-togethers she learned what the artsy crowd needed. That ranged from low-cost skills training to medical benefits. The result was her web business MediaBistro.com. She built it. She found funding to expand it. And eventually she sold it for millions. Touby is currently on sabbatical in Europe. When she returns she might be putting together the whatever for her next venture.

In 2005, I noticed there was no digital counterpart of the print Dominick Dunne who covered courtroom drama. For years I have been analyzing his mashup of bundling strong personal values, gossip, trusted sources, and going light on legal complexity. This was two years into my own journey away from being primarily a corporate ghostwriter/speechwiter and toward social media strategy and content.

On my own dime, I commuted the 90 minutes from my home office in Connecticut to the courthouse in downtown Providence, Rhode Island. There the four-month Rhode Island lead paint public nuisance trial was played out. I live-blogged it, leveraging in digital what I had picked up from Donne's print. That can be retrieved at http://janegenova.com under "legal."

Among the many many payoffs doing that, I learned how to "own" a territory. That territory does not just include journalistic-like coverage. It could be for a product, service, or a fresh approach to anything and everything. The rest is Genova the Barbarian, taking over areas which were or could have been controlled by old-line players.

We over-50 are not alone in having to produce our own income streams. But we have an edge. And an edge is a terrible thing to waste, particularly in an economy of scarcity versus the overflow-

INTRODUCTION

ing abundance of earlier times. The young, both in the U.S. and nations like Ireland and Spain, are having a brutal time getting in and staying in the workplace.

They lack our experience going to work. We know, for example, that employers and clients are hiring results, not a relationship. Hold the personality. We present ourselves on paper, through email, on-the-phone, and in-person as demonstrating we can do *that* specific job or assignment. No, we do not roll ourselves out generically.

We also know how to assess what is, what could be emerging, and what has been declining. That positions us to cash in on trends. Our employers and clients sense that. That makes us more valuable in their eyes. The new-economy game is about creating value.

In addition, we are all grown up, at least in the ways of the world. We can smell a scam, fad, or unneeded frill a mile away. No, we do not waste employers's, clients's or our own time in enthusiasms.

We discern what could yield results. When those results do not come, we leap in with course correction – confidently.

A third advantage is that we have outgrown most of youth's ego needs, including for excessive material rewards. By time we reach over-50, we have been able to calculate how much ego costs the workplace. It probably has cost us plenty ourselves in our own careers. Those include unnecessary errors of judgment, feuds, inability to let go, and obsession with compensation and perks. One might say: We over-50 are professionally all grown-up.

In addition, currently there are fewer of the constraints of aging.

◄ OVER-50: HOW WE KEEP WORKING

More work is cognitive and creative, not physical. Research shows that when it comes to cognitive learning, those 49-72 did as well as those 18-25, in terms of grades. There was the plus that the older group had a higher rate of completing the study programs [Source: California State University.]

The law is also on our side. About two years ago, the law firm Sidley Austin, in a lawsuit filed by the Equal Employment Opportunity Commission [EEOC], settled for $27.5 million with 32 partners. The complaint was age discrimination. The EEOC has been a tiger on the matter of aging. In January 2010, it filed a lawsuit against law firm Kelley Drye & Warren on behalf of a 79-year-old partner and "similarly situated employees." The complaint is age discrimination.

Yes, on one hand, we have plenty going for us. On the other, there are obstacles. They can be compressed for simplicity into two.

One is the mindset we had developed during predicable, affluent times. It is the expectation of progress, on all levels. We have come to assume that every aspect of our professional and personal lives will improve. The standard of living will continue to rise. We can debt-out the future. After all, inflation makes it foolish not to spend too much now and save too little. Eventually, we will bump into the right investment advisor for us, when we need to be thinking that way. No question, the ability to deal with disappointment, setbacks, and career catastrophe atrophied.

Of course, that assumption is complete delusion now. If we uttered it in front of family or friends, they would recommend that we "see a therapist." The only thing that seems to progress is our shrewdness about making a living.

INTRODUCTION

Sometimes that is all it will be: Just the ability to pay our bills.

Other times, it will be financial success beyond our wildest dreams. But there is nothing expected or automatic about it. We do it, every bit of it. We are responsible for making a living and how satisfying and lucrative that living will be.

The other constraint is the socialization some of us received in our Fortune 500 careers, professional-services firms, and upper-middle-class communities. The message was clear: Hustling was counterproductive to success. The ethos of WASP or elite grace, calm and seeming in control prevailed. We overheard the delighted gossip about so-and-so. He or she had not been offered the position or received the promotion or the assignment because of coming across way too hungry. Style was everything. It always trumped substance. Business wanted to appear classy. It did not someone it perceived as "rough around the edges," "working class," or "trying too hard."

Currently, we have to break a sweat. What we are learning is not to bother ourselves one bit about who sees us going after what we want. Professional self-consciousness has gone the way of the DOS operating system. We over-50 are the generation who embrace the wisdom of Henry Ford I. He observed that we never complain and we never explain. Right now we do not explain that, yes, we are hungry. It is no one else's business. It is, yes, our business, literally. We may appear rough around the edges, working class, and trying too hard. Employers and clients *love* to see that.

In this book we will deal with these advantages, obstacles, and more. Those who have read drafts of the book have told me that it will be the dog-eared bible for those over-50 who intend to keep working. Specifically, what will we gain in insight and behavior change from this book? Here are some of those takeaways:

- ✓ Moving more easily from the past to the now. Being in the present gets us to the future. Being in the past gets us labeled as "old."

- ✓ Developing the habit of going-for-it. That is the essence of hustle: Spotting, pouncing on, and exploiting opportunity.

- ✓ Moving forward without narrowly defined goals. When we are waiting for X to happen, we may miss that Y is opening up to be significant market space.

- ✓ Unbundling work from all the baggage it has taken on since World War II. That has included demanding from it meaning, status, sense of belonging, and even a possible vocation or "calling."

Who can have these kinds of takeaways? All of us. That is even though we are hardly homogeneous.

Some of did not skip a beat in pursuing a marketable degree such as an M.D. or M.B.A. and following an upward trajectory.

Some of us took time out for radical politics and roads less traveled.

Some have already changed careers once or twice.

Some took their degrees to the suburbs and reared family. Many of them are re-entering the workforce.

INTRODUCTION

Some made outstanding livings as plumbers and electricians.

Some have spent whole careers in one line of work such as journalism, law or human resources and have to transition to other fields.

Some have retired and returned to the work world.

What we all have in common is that we came of age in affluence and success appeared the result of careful planning and taking on the necessary protective coloring, with smoothness and class. Our challenge is to change just about everything we assumed and did to make a good living. The good news is that change is not that tough a nut to crack.

We can supplement what we read here on digital sites http://over-50.typepad.com and http://careertransitions.typepad.com.

CHAPTER 1

Black Swans: Humans plan, the gods laugh

Centuries before the current economic volatility there was a treasured Yiddish saying: *"Menschen tracht und Gott Lacht."* That translated into "Humans plan, the gods laugh." It was recognition that often what happens is not what we plan.

The extension of that wisdom, particularly, for our current professional life, is that if we cling to our plans too tightly, we will not spot opportunity, connect the dots, and plow in the resources to pursue it.

Steve Jobs never completed The Plan to finish college. Instead he created Apple. Bill Gates did not complete The Plan to finish at Harvard. Instead he started Microsoft. Hillary Clinton never did get to the White House, on her own. But she leveraged the influence and power acquired during that run to become Secretary of State. Supposed she had sulked after her original plan did not work out and went into political exile?

Plans have become more fantasy items that strategies. Not that fantasy is a bad thing. It was wired into our brains to help us eventually cope with what is. Fantasy provides a free vacation for life.

OVER-50: HOW WE KEEP WORKING

In general, plans are nothing but fantasy items.

Many of us are finally getting that about those detailed plans we have for ourselves, our businesses, our children, and even for their children. That is primarily thanks to financial-markets expert Nassim Taleb. He brought mainstream the concept of "The Black Swan" with his best-selling book by that title. Blacks Swans are those unexpected developments, such as the Internet, which have profound unexpected consequences. The classic example is how the Internet wiped out industries and is the platform for launching new ones. Talk about Creative Destruction.

The powers-that-be at publishing empire Conde Nast treated VANITY FAIR as one of its star brands. It was on the VANITY FAIR brandname that the company hosted the hot Oscar parties. Writers whose investigative reporting appeared in the publication were made. Then the company had called in management consultant firm McKinsey to reset it for a digital age. It is up to Conde Nast if it is willing to change enough to transform the Internet from a near-death experience to an opportunity. The February 2010 edition of VANITY FAIR was light on ads. But the powers-that-be might be learning something. The March 2010 edition was back to its usual weight. There were plenty of those ads for luxury items.

Simultaneously, not only are external factors in upheaval, so are we who are over-50. No one gets through a half century, at least not the half we have been through, without a mixed bag of wonderful and awful. At some point we have to digest that. After we do, we are, as they say, "changed," "re-born," "enlightened," "wiser but sadder," "smarter businesspeople," and "all business." We are not the professionals we were in our 30s and 40s. Too much has happened and those of us who sorted that too much out have become very different kinds of professionals. That is usually in our favor.

BLACK SWANS: HUMANS PLAN, THE GODS LAUGH ➤

Singer/songwriter Leonard Cohen had been so successful that he took a break to stay in a Buddhist monastery. After he had found the inner peace he was searching for he returned to his life. It was then that he found out that his manager had embezzled his millions. At an age when most entertainers are long retired Cohen *had to* return to work. At first that was a keen disappointment. Then he went on to a fresh new level in his art. In the January 2007 edition of the Buddhist publication SHAMBHALA SUN, Pico Iyer writes, *"The shock and excitement of the new work comes, in part, from the fact that some parts are written – and delivered – in a female voice."*

Prince Hal type son of power and privilege George W. Bush became a two-term president, who is still vilified even by some in his own party. But, in these times of the Black Swan we do not count him out. A positive form of the Black Swan can sweep him back into influence and power. Just consider discredited former president Jimmy Carter who has rebuilt his reputation as a philanthropist.

One-time junk-bond king Michael Milikin went from unprecedented wealth to prison. He is currently a respected philanthropist.

Economist and one-time head of the Federal Reserve Paul Volcker was the punching bag for folk hero Lee Iacocca when Chrysler was being turned around in the early 1980s. In late 2009 he was being consulted by the Obama Administration as the voice of economic reason.

Another economist Larry Summers was encouraged to leave the presidency of Harvard University. He popped back up in the Obama Administration.

And who knows what Hillary Clinton, currently Secretary of State,

◄ OVER-50: HOW WE KEEP WORKING

and her husband Bill Clinton, a former two-term president, will be up to next.

At one time these kinds of wide and winding career roads would have been unusual. In the 21st century they are typical. Surprises, shocks are built into the metabolism of our era.

So, as Black Swans visit our careers and personal lives, we wake up one morning and know in our gut we are not the professional or person we had been. We may recognize that wealth might not be the way we are going to keep score any more. This marriage might no longer be for us. Perhaps we realize we are more on the entrepreneurial side than the organization man or woman. We might have a solid idea for a business and have to figure out the financing. We yearn for a dog, a shack in Maine, a boy toy, a second family, a daughter who would just get married.

Fortunately, we have lots of company. We are not going through this outer and inner reset alone. Most of us can send an email to another over-50 and we are immediately on the same wavelength about what might be happening around us and within us.

Most of us have come to agree that *how* we go about making a living had been set on its ear. It is opportunistic, not linear, not happening in a carefully planned straight-line fashion. No, these are not our fathers's or mentors's versions of doing well.

Yet, this has not been easy, has it. The odds may be on our side for success but at what cost? The world we had come to expect in the mature phases of our professional life is no where to be found.

Can the new way of the world become less scary and more of an adventure? Yes.

BLACK SWANS: HUMANS PLAN, THE GODS LAUGH

WHAT WE THINK WE KNOW:

- ❖ Planning in too much detail and too far into the future can conceal from us current opportunities. In a sense planning has become a form of fantasy, or free vacation for the work world as it is.

- ❖ Our era is now bulging with role models who can show us the new way of succeeding. They include U.S. Senator from Massachusetts Scott Brown, Cirque du Soleil Chief Executive Officer Guy Laiberte, U.S. Representative Patrick Kennedy who had the courage not to run for re-election, and aide to John Edwards Andrew Young who turned a lemon into lemonade. We may not approve of all these roads being traveled. But we have to admit they are leading from the past into a now.

- ❖ We all assumed that our professional life would become easier. It has not. It will not. Yes, we can manage that.

CHAPTER 2

We Like This Job: How to hold onto it

Some of us have been at the same organization or even the same job in that organization for a long time. We want to keep it that way. The pay and perks are good. We like what we do. There are opportunities to continue to learn. Those of us who have managed this – and it is not easy – understand what it takes to hold onto to a job and perhaps even receive promotions over-50.

Who are these Settlers-In?

They include over-50 Paul Michael Pohl at Jones Day Law Firm. He had been the Managing Partner of the Pittsburgh office, now he is the Global Head of Product Liability. Over a year ago his defense team was able to have the Rhode Island Supreme Court toss the lead paint public nuisance case against client Sherwin-Williams. The legal media hail Pohl as a worldwide rainmaker. He knows *everyone*, including Prince Charles.

There is Richard Kosmicki, the Head of Media Relations at The Dilenschneider Group in Manhattan. He is in his 80s. His expertise is that hard-to-reach old or print media such as the reporters and editors at THE WALL STREET JOURNAL. Daily he boards the train in Westport, Connecticut [just like Thomas E. Rath did in Sloan Wilson's "The Man In The Gray Flannel Suit"] and rides into Grand Central in Manhattan. Then he takes the set of elevators up to the 26th floor. When darkness settles on the city he takes the elevator down and returns home.

There is Joanne Boyle, President of Seton Hill University, Greensburg, Pennsylvania. She took that job in the later 1980s. On her watch this one-time all-women's college I graduated from was transformed into a coed university and a community resource. For example, the university hosted lectures by Harvard Business Professor Rosabeth Kanter and spiritual leader the Dalai Lama. Boyle is about a decade older than I am so that puts her in her 70s.

In the U.S. Senate there is Robert Byrd from West Virginia. In his ninth decade, he maintains power, despite on-and-off-again health.

What might be the secret of job longevity? Actually, there are secrets. And they tend to be idiosyncratic. Everyone who manages to hold on in the same organization seems to have fitted their survival style to the specific soul of that entity. But there are general things which we have observed about this phenomenon. These may or may not apply to the professionals mentioned earlier.

The Settlers-In Bible:

Being There. People want their leaders, employees, and vendors to be there. There seems to be something hardwired in the human psyche which needs to have those who lead us, serve us, or just make us feel a certain way present. Inside the Beltway, lots of folks used to cluck "Where's Mrs. Kennedy?" during the early days of that Administration. She preferred being elsewhere and the city did not like that. At Yale, the students tended to chant the same thing about its one-time President Benno C. Schmidt, Jr. He was not around enough. He did not hold that job all that long.

Be there and the mob will think long and hard before tossing us out on our ear. They remember if we were or were not there today, not the three straight months we were there 80 hours a week. Incidentally, organizations tend to purchase from the last vendor who pitched to them and followed up.

Accessibility. There is a line between being approachable and being too porous. Stayers intuitively know how to stay on the right side of that line. They invite others in. They listen. They make sure we are aware that they are considering our recommendation or investigating our concern. But there is an invisible barrier which keeps nuisances out. That sends the message of power. That also lets others know they know their own worth. Research and experience both show that salesmen who respect themselves and therefore their time tend to close more often and on more than those who allow prospects to walk all over them.

The Favor Bank. Getting things done, along with reinforcing one's position, requires plenty of cooperation. That is facilitated easily through what is known as The Favor Bank. Players encourage others to set up an account and make withdrawals. That puts them in debt. Those debts can be called in when the survivors need something to get done. Maybe the employer wants his teenage son admitted to a private prep. The client wants warning if BLOOMBERG BUSINESS WEEK is doing a negative article on her company. The colleague needs reassurance he is not going to jail.

It is sometimes said that The Favor Bank is a prerequisite to power. Without it, there can be no power base.

Sustained Performance. Few argue with results. Even our most vocal critics as well as downright enemies have to concede that things get accomplished. In a sense that is the best kind of job insurance. We continue to pile on positive outcomes and maintain a low percentage of what never gets done.

That is not enough, though. We promote those results. The best way of doing that is through third parties, not ourselves. Those third parties include the media, organizations which recognize what we do, and allies who plant positive buzz about our accomplishments.

Knowing Secrets. When the survivor is the holder of others's secrets, there is little motivation to rock the boat. Do that and the secrets could wash overboard. The crude way of referring to this job protection is: Knowing where the bodies are buried.

That is why it is a reckless move to pen a tell-all as former John Edwards's aide Andrew Young did. He will earn money from the book per se. But he is preventing himself from making a platform for a new career path. No one likes a snitch. More importantly no one trusts as snitch. Even respected whistleblowers have difficulty earning a living post-disclosure.

Holding Key Pieces of Operations/Being the Brand. Some organizations strive to make no one indispensable. That used to be how corporate America operated in the age of affluence. There was built-in redundancy. There was at least one or more who could parachute in and do our functions. That ended in the late 1980s. When Kraft conducted layoffs in Rye Brook, New York, there was even the use of the term "redundancy." It was eliminating that. Survivors seem to ensure there are aspects of their functions not easily performed by others. These could range from symbolic rituals to their deep networks to funding sources.

In addition, survivors understand how to make themselves part or all of the brand. The powers-that-be have their branding down cold. They will hesitate to tamper with an organization's brand identity.

Source of work. Survivors can distribute work to others. This ability becomes increasingly important as work becomes not so easy to obtain.

This was exactly the way machine politics went. If we in Jersey City, New Jersey, known for Frank Hague ward politics, supported the right people, we could expect to always have a job. Some were patronage positions, others were because the mayor's mother knew our brother and so we got an interview at a local organization.

Not all of us want to be those kinds of survivors. We have no desire to stay in one organization or one job or be promoted in that organization to another job. However, we can learn plenty by their moves. If we want to preserve anything, be it a flow of work, a network, a marriage, a close relationship with our children, we have to operate strategically and with constant vigilance. Nothing just happens. If we take our eye off what is going on, we could easily lose everything, quickly. The best analogy for that is supervising a toddler. Blink our eyes and the kid is out the door, in traffic.

WHAT WE THINK WE KNOW:

- ❖ Those who maintain positions in organizations and even

get promoted put their unique imprint on that job. Each instance of survival could make for a case study.

❖ However, there are commonalities in tactics, ranging from simply being there to ensuring ongoing outcomes to not being easily replaceable.

❖ Preserving anything, be it a job, network, marriage, or relationship with a son or daughter, requires strategy and vigilance.

CHAPTER 3

Finding Our Next Job, Assignment, Or Business Venture

Steve McQueen had no education. His mother was a prostitute and alcoholic. She could not care for him and could not make up her mind whether she even cared about him. The father? Left and never to be found, athough McQueen had tried. Yet, this boy-man never failed to come up with a way to make a living until he stumbled into acting. And when he did his acting he brought all those earlier experiences to bear.

Darwin Porter's 2009 biography "Steve McQueen King of Cool" tells us all that. When I read it I became convinced that McQueen's ways of staying economically whole, even when he emotionally was not, could be models for how we can start over.

Maybe our profession, like human resources, had hit such hard times that it is obvious there is not much for us there any more. If we want another manufacturing executive position we would have to move our families south, and with a steep cut in compensation. Journalists are making about a buck an hour freelancing for the writing mills. Perhaps we are deep-fried from too much travel and then weeks in a hotel in Japan. Or we bite the bullet and recognize, after three decades in product liability law, we never liked law in the first place.

We come to that fork in the road. Then we ask: How do we find and try on The Next?

That starts with an exhaustive inventory of our natural abilities such as mechanical, learned skills, knowledge bases, personality traits, and professional experience going back all the way to grade school when we fundraised by hawking subscriptions for the local newspaper. Add to that if we moonlighted in the family businesses, was the nanny who was the mother's secret weapon, and popped the corn at the movie theatre.

Next, we observe the patterns. Do we continue to go back to one line of work, either to earn decent money or simply out of love of what it is we do? Do we flee other lines of work, no matter how secure they were or how much they paid? What experiences provided us good memories and which bad? Although we never were paid salespeople perhaps that is where our natural ability is. Did working with our entrepreneurial family make us feel safe and needed? Do we excel at tasks done with our hands rather than challenges involving navigating organizational politics?

As confused as McQeen was, he knew what could earn him a buck and make his employer happy. On interviews he would declare that he would have any mechanical job down within two weeks. And he did. We can know our marketable abilities in the same confident way. It was McQueen's sureness that helped land him those jobs.

At this point we make what might be labeled The Promising List.

FINDING OUR NEXT JOB, ASSIGNMENT, OR BUSINESS VENTURE

It contains whatever we can use from ourselves and our background that we can sense we can put out there to make a living. Then it is time for some serious homework.

We turn on the job boards. We can start with Craigslist help-wanted for our hometown in New Haven, Connecticut. We go through all the categories, reading the job descriptions and what is required. We match them to what is on our list.

Then we check out what we consider we might be able to market in those categories on other job boards such as Monster.com and Careerbuilder.com. We focus on what language the employers or clients are using, what is required, and what is a plus.

The fastest and easiest way in is through temporary assignments, freelance work, and part-time jobs. At this point, we could create our presentation materials such as resumes and cover letters. Those how-tos are explained in later chapters in this book.

But, not so fast, we figure. We tend to be highly educated so we feel we need to collect more information. We research the fields. We can obtain some high-powered information if we make an appointment with the admissions and career departments at universities and trade schools in those lines of work. We cold-call a few folks the yellow pages, print or digital, list as working in those fields. We ask 20 minutes of their time.

So far, so good? It is then that we will go about creating resumes for ourselves. If we need more experience than we already have in those areas we go out and get it. For marketing communications in the mid 1990s, I knocked on the doors of businesses in downtown Stamford, Connecticut. Of course, they took the offer of free promotional materials. Some hit the jackpot using them. I got a full-time job at CIGNA in, yes, marketing communications.

Or we might launch a business in the category. The best approach is a combination of a part-time job and the startup. We learn from both, simultaneously.

Some others are not so methodical. They just jump into something new. They hear that the web gift-basket company needs B2B salespeople. It is straight commission so the company does not lose in hiring cold. In back of their minds is to establish a more creative version of that approach.

We hear at the bar about how some children are struggling in science courses at their middle school. We research the tutoring rates charged by centers already in business. We underprice those, create our brand, put up our website, place advertising everywhere, and contact appropriate third parties such as schools, child therapists, and parent online communities. The ham in us gets loose. We stage science shows at meetings of scout organizations, church youth groups, and county fairs. Soon we are hiring staff. Next, we are doing the legal work to franchise.

If we are feeling a sense of excitement as we read about these new ventures we should be. Applying our talents and wits out there and watching them grow money – it does not get better than that. Dominick Dunne reports that the happiest time of his life was when he was residing at the YMCA. He was attempting to change careers by entering the book-writing field. There at the YMCA, on the advice of media pro Tina Brown, he was composing a book about the court trial of his daughter's murderer. He was never that happy again. Incidentally, the book did prove to be the platform for Dunne 2.0.

FINDING OUR NEXT JOB, ASSIGNMENT, OR BUSINESS VENTURE

Yes, making a living can be an adventure. In some ways, we in America are returning to an earlier time in our national history. That was the age of the street hustler. My uncles were among them. Author Saul Bellow captured that in his 1949 novel "The Adventures of Augie March." March's philosophy of survival was coming up with a scheme. That sure was not the era of angst. Present a problem, hustlers like March applied imagination, energy and their knowledge of the world. And that was that. Hand-wringing? They never thought of it.

The current analogue of March is the loveable rascals like Alec Baldwin, Dave Letterman, and Bill Clinton. Their female counterparts are Paris Hilton, Ellen, and Sarah/Bristol Palin. We keep giving them more rope, not so we can wait for them to hang themselves, but so that they can delight us with their feats of cunning.

WHAT WE THINK WE KNOW:

- ❖ No one is too uneducated or emotionally a mess to make a living. Many are too educated and too preoccupied with their "issues" to make a go at starting over.

- ❖ Our future way to make a buck is locked in our past. That includes our natural abilities, personality traits, learned skills, knowledge bases, and experience.

- ❖ A little research about what is out there can have big payoffs.

- ❖ We are back in the era of the street hustler. That means we leverage imagination, energy and what we know about the world.

CHAPTER 4

Change, Stuck, Change, Stuck

Okay, we may have a job and have a hunch that we will be able to keep it. We may have made that transition to a new industry, company or business. We may be on our way to a new career path. However, we keep hearing that mandate: *Change or die.*

What does that mean for us, on an individual basis? Sure we recognize that IBM has to keep changing. It almost did die in the early 1990s.

However, when it comes to us, change seems less imperative, less urgent. But is it? This is what this chapter is about: Change and us.

First off, what do we have to change?

For most of us, that is our behavior. When we accomplish that, the rest such as our attitudes and values will fall into place. It is our behavior, not what we think, that keeps us working or precipitates our joining the breadline.

This chapter is about our behavior. Affluence gave us a bias *against* taking action. Wealth put the premium on analysis, report-writing, and feeling comfortable in the life of the mind. Action seemed to be for the serfs, those mid-level creatures who implement our grand plans. That is precisely why the book "In Search of Excellence" was viewed in the early 1980s as providing such breakthroughs for business. It announced that smart companies *do things*. Some extended that to: *Smart people do things*.

The mandate was praised, used in executive speeches, and mouthed in the annual report. However, the business culture and our individual perspective continued to put the emphasis on analysis. For example, if we were failing or unhappy in our professional path, we were advised to consult with a career advisor, seek out therapy, hire an executive coach, and invest even more in that stuckness by studying for another degree such as an MBA or one in Information Technology. The message was: We can never be too cautious. Stay the course. Stay in our heads. *Stay stuck*.

With abundance gone as well as many traditional ways of making a good living, organizations and individuals are being forced to leave their comfort zone of studying a situation to death and taking a risk by taking action. That has not been feeling so hot. Action scares a lot of us, a lot.

That should not be a surprise. After all, the zeitgeist of the 21-century is fear. That powerful emotion is being discussed and researched more. It is so pervasive and such a potential source of moving us forward or freezing us in panic that even the most conventional scientific and management thinkers have stopped foisting the clichés on us about fear.

One of the more exciting books out there is the 2009 "Extreme Fear: The Science of Your Mind in Danger." It is by science journalist Jeff Wise. The author admits that fear remains a mysterious entity. That in itself is a big leap forward. We are not being told that we are being told the Platonic or universal truth about fear.

On the one hand fear can provide the focus, energy, and creativity to solve an urgent problem. The mother sweet-talks the carjacker to release her baby. The abused employee turns the table on the bullying boss by doing what it takes to file a class-action lawsuit. The solo pilot experiencing an anxiety attack identifies the inner terror as just that and follows normal flying procedures.

On the other hand, fear can so overwhelm us that we cannot perform effectively. The mugger attacks and we are frozen with fear. Our company is planning a Reduction-in-Force and we panic to the point of calling too much attention to ourselves. Our mortgage is under water and there seems no exit but suicide.

What Wise tells us is that scientific opinion about fear has gone beyond the fight or flight response. For example, scientists are indicating us that there are myriad ways to prevent ourselves from becoming so stressed-out that we cannot cope with fear. That usually entails practice, just the way an athlete or actor prepares for a flawless performance, no matter what might be taking place inside themselves or outside in the audience.

What do we practice?

One proven exercise is to simply become less self-conscious. We stop watching others watching us. We stay in the performance, even if it involves delivering a PowerPoint Presentation to a Board of Directors who, the grapevine has it, is not enthusiastic about our ideas. The sports world calls that staying in the zone. The creatives call it allowing The Flow. Fear specialists would call it managing the fear response. If we are totally engrossed in an activity, that provides a sealed compartment. Fear can not enter, at least not to the point of dominating.

Another exercise is to monitor how much fear is disabling us. After we make that assessment we can start on primitive course correction. That could be the simple process of breathing in, breathing out, with our concentration on taking those breaths. We could change the channel, as in picking up a book to read, flipping on the TV, walking down the corridor to distract ourselves with a conversation.

Longer term, we can research on the Internet and with our medical doctors medications which are targeted at the mechanisms which trigger severe anxiety. For example, some antidepressants, such as Zoloft, in the SSRI family block panic attacks. New forms of therapy such as Cognitive Behavioral Treatment develop the habit of taking action when fear becomes overwhelming. If we are engaged in activity, we are not feeling the fear so acutely.

There are also some of us who do not know that what we are feeling is fear. Therefore, we are left out there in the Darwinian jungle unaware that our decision-making might be based on fear we do not realize is taking us over like a monster from an alien universe. If we are in a downward trajectory, the prime mover on that might be fear. The best approach is an inventory of our emotional drivers. A free way of addressing fear and other disabling feelings is attending a 12-step program such as Emotions Anonymous or religious services. What seems to work here is surrendering to the reality that something – e.g. the fear – is beyond our control and is making our lives unmanageable.

However, fear is only one factor that inhibits change. Another is

CHANGE, STUCK, CHANGE, STUCK ❯

that most of us do not know how to go about change. Fortunately, the way has been simplified.

The heroes of that simplification process include Chip and Dan Heath. In 2007, those brothers gave us the breakthrough "Made to Stick: Why Some Ideas Survive and Others Die." Now they have given us their new book "Switch." It bulldozes through the assumed complexity and struggle of changing. The Heath Brothers provide us with simple levers to pull to get us on the right road.

They make this assertion: Small changes can have big impacts. After I read that I tried it out. I reside in a high-rise complex in New Haven, Connecticut. The development contains 1400 units. The constant chatter on the elevators, much of it directed at me in the form of neighborly conversation, was annoying. After all, my living depends on thinking about new approaches. A Hamlet type, all I could think was: Words, words, works.

Moving was the option that seemed most efficient. Then it dawned on me that such an approach might be like trying to kill a fly with a canon. Applying the Heath Brothers's reach toward simplicity, I decided to try out if wearing a pair of sunglasses would deter conversation. After all, there would be no eye contact. There would also be the bonus of presenting myself as a kind of outlier. No one else in the complex sported sunglasses year-round.

It did the trick. No only has all conversations stopped. I have become invisible. No one even acknowledges my presence on the elevators with a nod or body language. I can continue with building my new niche businesses without the disruption of moving, at least right now.

In "Switch," the Heath Brothers tell us that the problem of malnutrition in a Viet Nam village was solved without the usual exhaustive analysis. Instead, the focus was on identifying the bright spot or what was working. In that situation, the change agent went to the village and saw that, despite all the residents sharing the same socio-economic background, some families were not malnourished. Attention was put there. What were those families doing differently? The factors were found. Then a way was created to motivate other families to follow the program. Yeah, change happened that simply. Change also happened without relying on expert opinion. *We can do it.*

In short, what used to keep us stuck can now be dealt with. But there is more. Here are other recommendations to consider when we hear those words: *Change or die.*

Consider a professional identity as likely to be changed as a hairdo, a brand of clothing, or our favorite restaurant. That kind of change used to be thought of as a flip-flop personality. Those who engaged in modifying their persona often were vilified as lacking character and principles. They were labeled opportunists. When African-American New York leader Al Sharpton lost weight and presented himself as a more traditional kind of leader, many condemned him, Holden Caufield-like, as a phony.

Now, no matter what others think, we have to look at modifying our professional identity as commonplace as getting a new hairdo. Such as change has no character or moral import. It is a financial necessity. Hillary Clinton was way ahead of most of us on that one.

When Clinton was elected U.S. Senator, she was savvy enough to seek advice from BigFoot Robert Byrd. He told her two things: Be deferential and work hard. She did both. The first might have been an adjustment. The second was second-nature. When she got up to speed on being U.S. Secretary of State, she took on more a leadership persona, as well she should have.

After being hammered for appearing too cool, President Barack Obama is beginning to develop more of a statesmanlike persona. As the dust settles on the John Edwards's scandal, Elizabeth Edwards, once viewed and treated as Saint Elizabeth, will have to put together a fresh public image. It would include lessons brutally learned.

The time of greatest vulnerability is often when we are between these professional identities or personas. We might have left the profession of practicing law and now are employed as an aide to a Congressman. We do not have the game down in terms of the face to meet and greet other faces. For the interim, we have to craft a way to insulate ourselves from the worst out there. Usually that comes from communicating confidence but keeping ourselves protected through a reserved personality. No, we do not have to let everybody or anybody in. Friendliness is overrated in America.

The best way to learn what is appropriate, then what gives us the edge is to observe the winners and losers in our new fields. Deconstruct what they do and do not do. Imitate the winners, rid out menu of behaviors from what losers habitually do.

Be totally pragmatic about earning a living. Dump the baggage we used to make it carry.

In the 20th century, we became our jobs. Joanne B. Cuilla is an expert on the philosophy and psychology of work. Her 2000 book "The Working Life: The Promise and Betrayal of Modern

Work" describes all the abstractions and symbolism we attach to making a living.

For our career, for example, we demand or used to demand meaning, identity, connection to groups, and even often as sense of calling or a "vocation." If we are lugging all that from industry to industry we are lugging too much. No wonder change can seem like such a formidable undertaking.

Some of the most resistant to career transition are those who considered themselves with a vocation. At the top of the list are journalists. The lion's share are not stars and were underpaid. Yet, that mission they assumed they had is hard to replace. In Massachusetts there was a state program to retrain unemployed journalists. At the end they would probably earn more. However, some are still in mourning for what they had "lost."

There is no good reason to pile on abstractions to the already hard undertaking of making a living. My grandparents, parents, and uncles did not even dream of viewing work as anything but work. As a result, both when they were at work and when they were away from work, they lived a much fuller life than I have and wound up with a bundle to leave to their children. Perhaps that model should be given more respect.

Yes, the glass is really half full and that is a blessing. Many of the enduring templates for behavior change, ranging from Dale Carnegie Systems to Alcoholics Anonymous, include an attitude of gratitude. The mindset is two-fold.

One part is to view the glass as half full. The other is to be thankful for that half.

Of course, these incorporate the fundamentals of positive thinking. It may seem cliché or Pollyanna, but the reality is that a sunny humility breaks open opportunities. Resentment, regret, blaming are not selling.

Going from I-should-have/they-should-have to appreciation for what is in the now is not difficult. One piece is imitating the winners. Observe Michelle Obama, John Walsh, Daniel Goleman, recovered substance abusers, and Patrick Kennedy. The other piece is avoiding the self-defeating body language, facial expressions, language and behavior of the losers. Observe the chronically unemployed, the underemployed, active substance abusers, and isolated elderly.

We have every right and every economic reason to think for ourselves. There is so much call to return to intuition and instinct. That is because, well, we were essentially animals and there is plenty of danger in the forest. We better use those survival mechanisms we were born with and have developed further along the way.

It has come to this: Either we are lunch or we find lunch. There is nothing wrong with taking a peek at how experts view the world, the latest research, forecasts by government agencies, and futuristic speculation. However, opportunity comes down to our being able to see bits and pieces and then connecting the dots. Success results when we do that earlier or better or cheaper or with more style than others.

The more confused we are, the more advice we tend to invite. The solution is to end the confusion and try new things. Likely more things will not work than work. That is the new rite of passage. Failure is a gold mine of learning.

OVER-50: HOW WE KEEP WORKING

WHAT WE THINK WE KNOW:

- ❖ No matter how settled in we may assume we are in our jobs or business, how much transition we have already been through, or how strong we have become as a result of biting the bullet and changing, we will have to continue to change.

- ❖ Small changes can have big impacts.

- ❖ Fear can lead us to perform poorly. The good news is that there are ways to manage fear.

- ❖ Modifying our professional identity is no one's business but our own and it is our business.

CHAPTER 5

We Got To Want To Work

We can smell a needy person a mile away. Either we flee from or, more often, exploit that neediness. The needy are rarely hired. If they are hired for a job or a project it is because they can be overworked, tormented by the boss and clients, and never properly rewarded.

Neediness comes in many forms. Think the expression Poor Little Rich Boy. Brooke Astor's son Anthony Marshall was certainly needy. Both his mother and his wife Charlene seemed to push him around because of that. He had lost the ability to act on his own behalf and be self-protective.

When I was flush with cash flow and sitting on a fat 401K, I needed more and more success. That, of course, eventually deep-sixed my communications boutique. In 2003, I had to wake up and smell the reality that neediness is the kiss of death for all professionals.

The antithesis of neediness is the belief that we can get through whatever. We may emerge scarred. But we do get to that other side. That is because, explains Harvard Business School professor Rosabeth Kanter, we invest ourselves and other resources in getting out of a pickle or sustaining success. In her 2004 book "Confidence: How Winning Streaks & Losing Streaks Begin & End," Kanter notes that we use the term frequently but few of us understand what it entails.

Essentially, explains Kanter, confidence "helps people take control of circumstances rather than be dragged along by them." As scary an experience of losing it all in 2003 was, I somehow had the confidence that I would not only get through but be able to apply what I was learning to a fresh kind of career path.

The needy, on the other hand, often cry out like wounded animals in the jungle about needing work. Such behavior, obviously, does not communicate confidence. Secondly, with so many people lacking confidence, this is a kind of job applicant or vendor others have made it a policy not to hire.

How to shift from seeing ourselves and telling the world that we are needy to viewing ourselves and letting the marketplace know that we are in control?

The best lesson book for that has already been written by the growing number of comebacks. The first Baby Boomer president Bill Clinton tells readers in the January 2010 WIRED Magazine that when he lost out for a second term as governor in his state of Arkansas he regained his center – and confidence – by reverse-engineering his behavior. What he realized is that people perceived he had stopped listening. And he realized that they were right. Therefore, when he campaigned for the president his mantra was the sensitive "I feel your pain." His facial expressions and body language communicated that. The lesson here is that as soon as we make an effort to move from the space of defeat to try out other attitudes and behaviors we move from need to pursuing something we think we want. Others pick right up on that. They enjoy being part of our metamorphosis.

Another way out of need is financial realism. Often this takes a lot of getting used to.

The sixth-year associate laid off from a large Manhattan law firm will open a law office as a solo or with a few partners. That means mega changes. Those include ensuring fixed costs are rock bottom. That usually entails working from home with a Manhattan mail drop to create the impression of a real office. A little research will yield the information that as a member of the New York City Bar, the lawyer has access to the facility's conference room to meet with clients.

There will be no assistants. Any revenue coming in is desirable, even if the assignment is underpriced. One set of lawyers went out of business in a few months. They assessed as beneath them to take assignments from Craigslist which paid $50 an hour. After all, they had been used to so much more.

In addition, it might be necessary to have a day job or work for unrelated sources of revenue. While trying to establish a firm, the lawyer might also do temp work or walk dogs in Manhattan.

The legal example is just one of coming to terms with extreme pragmatism about money. Not needing money right this minute eliminates being needy. All we have to be focused on is paying our bills for today.

In extreme money pragmatism, renting trumps owning. As we age, there is a growing number of options for subsidized housing. Currently, I pay $620 monthly for 700-square feet, which includes a breathtaking view, parking space, as well as the heat, hot water, and electricity. Had I to pay the traditional rent for this view I have of Long Island Sound the monthly nut would be at least $2500.

As we exit the era of affluence, subsidized anything and everything is losing its stigma. The entity has been reconfigured as a blessing, a gift from the universe. My neighbors here in subsidized housing include a large number of those over-50 who go out every day to work. They are educated and comport themselves as middle-class. The former mayor of New Haven, Connecticut lives on my floor. Not one is sheepish about getting this kind of break on rent.

Home schooling makes expensive private school unnecessary. When I was selling my house in upper middle class West Hartford, Connecticut during the real estate boom, I demanded that first real estate agent be replaced. I ranted effectively. They assigned me the agency's second-best agent. And she certainly was that. She had achieved a good life for her family but not living in the pricey West Hartford area with its great school system. She lived in Hartford. There she home schooled her five children. That was smart. It still is smart for those who want to cut fixed costs.

Mass transportation eliminates the costs of maintaining an automobile and cars can be leased for business purposes. That is tax-deductible, of course. Last summer my car was stolen and eventually the insurance company declared it a total loss. The payment we negotiated was generous. I decided to not again take on the expense and worry of owning an auto. As a result, I have lost weight walking. More importantly I can listen to people's conversations on the bus and train. That has improved my writing. And not having a car to jump into provides more time for writing. I rent one of those Wrecks when I am paying for the car lease and one of those cars which are delivered to your home when the client is paying.

I haven't bought new in retail for several years. Consignment shops in upper middle class communities stock well-known brands, even in large sizes. One winter I found a coat, shoes, and sweater for $32 in a consignment shop in Seymour, Connecticut. Before the thrift shop burned down in North Haven, Connecticut I purchased a Coach purse for $40.

A third way to prevent being needy is a willingness to learn. It may seem overwhelming to an old print media representative to take the leap into new digital media. It is. But it turns out it is doable if we perform triage. We investigate what is the overview or the main points that are must-knows. This is available through inputting a few keywords into the Internet. We sit calmly and take it in. Then we have a sense of what specifics would provide the career runway we need. We take a course or teach ourselves. The libraries and bookstores have a growing number of how-to manuals. That cuts the cost from about $350 for a seminar to less than $30. Then we add to that knowledge base and skills. That is exactly how I was able to migrate from a traditional background in communications to social media.

The fourth path away from needy to abundant is to decouple ourselves from networks which no longer serve us. They may be professional trade associations, our alma mater, the agency we started out with, the particular meetings in White Plains, New York where we became sober, the service people we used for haircuts and dry cleaning, and the neighborhood watch committee. Those relationships can keep us frozen in a former professional identity.

No, we do not have to move to Mars. But we have to give ourselves the space to grow our new personas. Others either do not welcome our changes or become frightened by them and sabotage.

It takes room to get a plane in the air. It also takes room to get a second, third, or fourth act staged. Give ourselves that space and we will get the hang of never being needy again.

WHAT WE THINK WE KNOW:

- ❖ Neediness was never a welcome trait on the job market or in the search for new business. In the current Darwinian economy it is a downright nuisance.

- ❖ The way to attract employers and clients is by demonstrating we want the job or the project, *not need it*.

- ❖ We can avoid being needy by cutting fixed costs, learning new skills, and pruning networks from the past.

CHAPTER 6

We Are Our Stories: Those can be liabilities or assets

No surprise, public relations has become a high-growth field. By 2018, it is expected to increase its jobs by over 20 percent [Source: Bureau of Labor Statistics.] That is because of this: Public relations gurus are the experts who craft, promote, fine-tune, and overhaul our stories.

What are those stories? They range from what GM tells the car buyers, dealers and regulatory agencies about itself to what we communicate to prospective employers and clients.

There is more. Those stories are often the ones we wind up telling ourselves about ourselves. They are also what others have convinced us were or are the real scoop about us. In addition, the corridors of failure are full with those who believed what the media or sycophants told them about how brilliant they were. As management consultant Jim Collins explains in his 2009 book "How The Mighty Fall," taking that hype seriously can be a direct cause of a downward trajectory.

One more thing we have to know about stories. And that is that they are 100-percent man-made. Yet, there are too many of us who need to believe that stories have some kind of reality beyond the human-contrived entities they are. In Philosophy 101, we called that Platonism or the conviction that universal forms of our daily lives exist out there in the ether as permanent and the ultimate truth. In many religions, the essence of the almighty represents such a Platonic notion.

The problem with that Platonism, and there is a big problem with it, is that we become preoccupied with capturing the truth. Digging for it. Spending years in psychotherapy analyzing it and its implications. Yet, investing all that belief, commitment, and energy prevents us from creating stories which fit the specific need of an employer or client. Instead of aligning our credentials and the in-person presentation of self to applying for a job as a public relations professional, we stick to what we consider the "truth" about ourselves, our background, our temperament.

In short. our stories can hurt us. Frequently they do.

Or our stories can help us. And just as frequently they do.

See, stories directly shape how the world perceives and treats us and how we perceive and treat ourselves. Stories can limit us or expand our brand. They can hold us hostage to family myths, the mischief of enemies, and the past. They can also provide a fresh platform to build a more contemporary and more lucrative professional future.

A woman with a law degree and a graduate business degree came to me for a complimentary consultation about coaching. We both were to decide if one-on-one sessions would be useful

WE ARE OUR STORIES: THOSE CAN BE LIABILITIES OR ASSET

in her job search.

This 26-year-old woman introduced herself on the phone by saying, "I graduated from a second-rate law school, in the middle of the class." It was April and she had graduated the previous May, had passed the bar in Connecticut, and had not found a position practicing law. She told me that the career-placement staff at her alma mater ducked when she came in. They did not seem to want to deal with those finding it difficult to find work in their field. This kind of blaming-the-victim behavior, I have found, is typical in fields with declining manpower needs.

I reviewed her resume and asked, "Why are not telling me about your MBA? You offer employers and their clients a knowledge about business." That was all it took. In her interview the next day in Manhattan I advised her to begin her story this way, "The edge I bring this firm and your clients is that I know business. In addition to my law degree, and passing the bar exam, I have an MBA." She got the offer. No need for a single coaching session.

A 43-year-old former female executive in corporate marketing called me. "I was fired. That is holding me back from getting a comparable job in my field." She wondered what she should do. I spent the next 15 minutes of the complimentary consultation getting to know her strengths.

It was obvious she was an entrepreneurial type, not The Professional Woman or an old-line Organization "Man." "Change your story," I told her. The new lead-in, both in how she talked to herself and introduced herself to employers and clients, would be, "My DNA is entrepreneurial. That has meant that the results I produce come in beyond expectations, and under budget. Is that what you need?"

OVER-50: HOW WE KEEP WORKING

This woman bit the bullet and decided most corporate settings were not a good fit for her. She found a full-time position with benefits at a mid-sized marketing agency in the Midwest. She is learning what she can about operating a business and will eventually go out on her own. Yes, become an entrepreneur.

A 67-year-old man I met socially told me that he was managing a tax-preparation office. Then he proceeded to hold the group spellbound when he recounted how a woman the branch had done taxes for during five years went from earning $35,000 to seven figures. It was only after I encountered him several times that he told the rest of his story. He had been a middle-manager in Hewlett-Packard and had been laid-off. By then, I had already formed a perception of him as a winner. His timing was right on the reality of what kinds of information to release when and how.

No question, we need to listen to the stories we tell the world and ourselves and which we allow the world to tell about us. If we do not take control of the story, someone else, usually not with our best interests at heart, will.

How do we listen? Answer: With a pragmatic need to have that story present us in the most effective manner. This is not an exercise in craftsmanship. This is about earning a living.

Some tape record how we present ourselves over the phone and in-person. Some collect a representative sample of our emails, resumes, cover letters, tweets, blog posts, and books. Some seek out psychotherapy or a self-help program to capture those internal voices, often called the "terrorists within."

What we all then do is ask: Hey, is this the way self-caring, self-protective, ambitious professionals present themselves? What we

WE ARE OUR STORIES: THOSE CAN BE LIABILITIES OR ASSET ❧

have to look for includes:

Self-hate. Capitalism seems to operate by making us feel less than or never good enough. That drives us to work harder and grab at more and more symbols of success. Inevitably, there is an epidemic of self-hate among America's best and brightest. Buddhist monks pick this up right away. That embedded conviction of self-loathing deep-sixes our ability to truly prosper. If our stories resonate with not liking ourselves buyers hear it loud and clear.

The past. Nothing sticks on us like the past, whether it was good or bad. Yet, opportunity unfolds in the present. Prospects want to know what we can do for them this nanosecond.

Ambivalence. It may be necessary to leave our career path in law or management consulting. The obstacle is that part of us is still there. That shows. It screams to those in the next profession not to hire us. We are not ready for the move.

Fear. Although a universal emotion, fear is an entity which competent professionals know how to master. Signs of it either lead to not being hired or to the buyer to torment us.

Immaturity. Those parts of us which have not yet grown up frequently rear their heads in crisis or transition. This is an excellent chance to address those areas which need development. Yes, that is called Doing Work On Ourselves. This kind of work is no longer an option, not if we want to keep working. A neighbor gives me feedback on areas I must continue to work on. I treat her to Red Lobster and she gently informs me about areas requiring improvement. One has been my tendency, when nervous, to talk too fast and too loud.

Apology. That MBA we did not get, that law degree we did get, the job we did not take, the job we did take. The message this delivers to prospects is that we have not finished dealing with our past. No one wants to hear about that, particularly if they are paying for our time. Those decisions made in the past should stay in the past. Even if we have learned plenty from them, few want to be held hostage to the details. In telling our story, less is more.

How do change the stories that would help us reach our career goals, including obtaining a promotion?

Usually, we have to move into that territory slowly, at least if we are remaining in the same organization, networks, and neighborhood. Face it. In this Darwinian economy, few encourage our efforts to improve how we present ourselves. In addition, few welcome change in us. For both these reasons, if our change is too noticeable, we can expect sabotage, ridicule, interrogation, or even public criticism.

Remember that most celebrities are frozen in their identities because their fans will not allow them to change. That can extend to their wanting to introduce new songs, new character types in their acting, and in signature or branding. Demi Moore cannot become anything else. Fortunately, we can. But we have to manage that carefully.

What we focus on is only what needs to be adjusted. We focus on only what is blocking our professional mobility, at this time. We do not and should not aim to overhaul who we are. That is the first item of "business" that Buddhist nun Pema Chodron communicates to those wanting relief from their spiritual aches and pains. In her book "The Wisdom of No Escape," Chodron says, *"Meditation practice isn't about trying to throw ourselves away*

WE ARE OUR STORIES: THOSE CAN BE LIABILITIES OR ASSET ❧

and become something better. It's about befriending who we are already."

Most of us know at some level that some attitudes and behaviors have to go. The hard part is coming up with the courage to change. What helps so much there is studying others who have also gone that road less traveled.

In 2003, when my career path had collapsed and I was still working survival jobs, I read everything I could put my hands on about Dominick Dunne's comeback at age 50. For about six years what he did and did not do became guidelines to me. Here is what I got out of that Dominick Dunne self-help course:

- √ Admit something got us into trouble and change that one thing. For Dunne it was his arrogance, which had led to boasting and that in turn alienated those who could have helped him. For me, that tragic flaw was my lack of confidence. As a result my story tended to make others doubt my ability. As they teach in 12-step programs, I faked it [confidence] until I actually acquired it. With each victory, I did acquire a little of it.

- √ Listen. Dunne listened when literary star Tina Brown recommended that he publish a book on his attendance at his daughter's murder trial. That started off his new career as an out-of-the-box story-teller at criminal trials. I listened when cognitive behavioral therapist Amy Karnilowicz suggested I write about how I wound up in career lost and found. That led to blogging about that experience, which attracted business for my communications services. That, in turn, led to my coaching and then workshops. Along the way, I published my first novel "The Fat Guy From

Greenwich." It also dealt with that general career topic.

- √ Prune the network. Dunne created a whole new circle of allies. He left the social and professional wreckage of the past behind. Those from the past, I had decided, were probably part of the reason I got into the pickle I was in. I cut them off. Had to.

- √ Share our story with those who are still suffering. Dunne enhanced his ability to relate to sources by bonding with their pain. My biggest breakthroughs professionally have come through helping others through what I knew from my own experience.

Both the larger world and our own smaller worlds are filled with those who were held back by bad story-telling and broke free. In a sense, they have been put there for us.

What also can be useful in changing our stories is rewarding ourselves for "good behavior." When I went for three weeks without vomiting up my lack of confidence, I treated myself to a theatre performance.

In the next chapters we will look at different forms of professional stories: Resumes, cover letters, and interviews.

WHAT WE THINK WE KNOW:

- ❖ The stories we tell the world and to ourselves shape our success and failure. To be our own best public relations agent, we will ensure those stories highlight our strengths.

WE ARE OUR STORIES: THOSE CAN BE LIABILITIES OR ASSET

- ❖ Stories are man-made. Those narratives have no existence outside the human realm. We made them. We can change them. We should change them to help us keep working.

- ❖ Periodically we review our stories to find which no longer fit, which need to be compressed, and which reflect the self-hate we might have felt toward ourselves.

- ❖ Essentially, we are okay. We are focusing on parts of ourselves. This is not an extreme makeover.

CHAPTER 7

Resumes Tell Employers Stories They Want To Hear

Resumes — and yes, they should be plural — are not our story. They tell buyers, be they employers, clients, or customers, the stories they want to hear. Those stories have to perfectly aligned with what the particular job or assignment requires. That means that a lot of what is a pattern resume we are considering using will wind up on the cutting room floor. Any information in a resume which does not add to the story told to buyers has to go. It could provide buyers with a reason to reject us.

See, hiring is a high-risk project. A wrong pick can cost thousands, even millions, of dollars, plus lost time and negative publicity. Therefore, buyers need to be reassured by what is in the resume that they are hiring the right person. Increasingly skittish in this volatile economy, they are looking for every reason to knock us out of the box. That reason could be an elite school or a non-elite school, too much experience, not enough experience, too many career paths, only one career path, too many employers, only one employer, too many volunteer activities, too few altruistic pursuits.

◄ OVER-50: HOW WE KEEP WORKING

That is why if what we are going after is important to us we have to do two things: Research the organization as to its culture, recent history, its goals, and its manpower needs The other is to speedread the ad and the players for insight into hidden agendas. Based on what we derive from those, we will get one of our pattern resumes custom-made for that opportunity.

Yes, the game is playing to a very narrow audience. This is not mass marketing. It is micro-targeting.

The overall format of the resume depends on what is preferred in that industry or company. That is easily found out. Contact a head hunter for that field or even the human resources department of the organization. Ask which of the many types of resumes is most acceptable to them. In bookstores and libraries there are detailed instructions on how to create that kind of resume.

For us over-50 the general guidelines include:

√ Limit the professional history to about the last 10 years. If we have been self-employed for 20, that is irrelevant. List the past 10.

√ Leave dates of graduation off. It used to be that the organization's internal applications, including on the web, would require those dates. Enough people must have complained about age discrimination for most to discontinue that practice. There will be situations in which we have "too many" degrees. Father forgive me, but I advise some professionals to not list all those. Such information could scream: Insecure, so spent too much time in formal schooling.

RESUMES TELL EMPLOYERS STORIES THEY WANT TO HEAR

√ A video trailer might not be the best approach for the initial cut, if it includes a photo of us. That could communicate our age before the organization has a chance to assess what unique value we can bring. If the trailer simply captures how we work or a project we are engaged in, then it could be a plus.

√ The more concrete we can make results we have achieved and are achieving, the more persuasive. Most persuasive is the quantitative. "In seven months, the team reduced the breakeven point 48 percent."

√ Leadership positions are important. A useful item could be "As member of the American Marketing Association Regional Board I participated in change of national bylaws."

√ No need to mention a career change unless it was within the last 10 years. No one cares that my original career track had been to become a university humanities professor.

√ Negatives can be transformed into positives. When we were in prison we created a digital literacy program in which more than 400 inmates have participated in and 90 early releases now work with. In this case we are applying for a consulting position with a non-profit or the foundation of a corporation.

√ Gaps in employment history have to be filled, even if it is a force-fit. The usual cover story is consulting, operating a family business after the owner died, or attempting a start-up. What matters to buyers is that we understand the system well enough to know we have to provide a cover story. No organization wants a capitalist virgin.

√ Less can be more. We tend to create resumes which are way too extensive. That in itself tends to make us appear "old" and even out-of-touch.

Based on feedback we will keep fine-tuning each pattern resume and the specifics we provide on how it is customized. That is why the numbers game is recommended. We should apply to everything we can in order to test-market every aspect of our campaign. When we receive zero response, we can be assured that some or all aspects of my presentation materials are faulty.

FAQs:

Should a resume have a Summary Section?

That depends. This tends to be going out of fashion. It takes up space and usually says not much that is useful. Also, it can box us into seeming naïve, as when we state, "Seeking a challenging job in the marketing industry." Too many on LinkedIn present themselves in that generic manner. I sense that it hurts, not helps them.

However it can be useful if there is any ambiguity about what exactly we are applying for or what skill set we are emphasizing. Recently a teacher obtained a Master's Degree in Special Education. Because she was well known in school districts for her elementary school experience, the summary flagged that she was pursuing a position in her new field, that is Special Education.

Is lying ever okay?

RESUMES TELL EMPLOYERS STORIES THEY WANT TO HEAR

A falsehood is never okay. If detected, it can destroy our careers. What is okay is to present the data in the best light or to at least provide an explanation for them. For example if we left college and did not finish our degree we might state, "Emergency leave to take over the family business after my father died."

There is currently prejudice against those only employed by one company. How to fix this?

Even though employed by one company, we likely performed diverse tasks in it. With bullet points, indicate the various positions, describe the nature of the jobs including the number supervised, and indicate developmental milestones such as assisting during a turnover, and highlight concrete accomplishments. If there were promotions, highlight those.

In addition, we can mention other kinds of tasks we did in addition to working for that one employer. Did we freelance? Start a business? Bring a community sports team to victory? Publish? Deliver keynote speeches?

There can be prejudice against the self-employed seeking full-time employment. How to get around that?

The issue here is whether we can fit into an organization and be team players. Therefore, on the resume demonstrate partnerships with clients, cooperative ventures, and if we worked onsite at clients's facilities. The line between entrepreneur and employee is blurring. Therefore, having been an entrepreneur could give us an edge with an organization which needs more of that approach.

Does it pay to have a resume done professionally?

OVER-50: HOW WE KEEP WORKING

Not all of us have communications savvy. Most of us try first a Do-it-yourself approach. If that is not receiving a response, going to a professional might be worth it. Quality of those services varies. Ask around for recommendations. Interview service providers about how they go about creating resumes for particular industries, professions, and companies.

WHAT WE THINK WE KNOW:

- ❖ Resumes are employers, not for us. They are the audience. We create the stories they need to hear. Those stories are custom-made for each application which is important to us. If we are not getting a response we are doing something very wrong.

- ❖ Every word, sentence, and category of the resume has to align with the specific need of that employer or prospect. Whatever does not provides reason for the reader to toss it.

- ❖ Lying is never okay. What is more than okay, it is recommended, is to position the facts to compel the reader to pay attention. Yes, we want to elicit a WOW response.

- ❖ The resume will be aligned with all the rest of the promotional materials and the self we present at the interviews. Otherwise the buyer is confused. We do not want that. There should be a consistent story communicated.

CHAPTER 8

Cover Letters as Performance Art

Our cover letter puts in play a process. That process is a form of performance art. It sets the stage for us to introduce ourselves to buyers. They can choose to "meet" us or not. If they keep refusing to "meet" us when we send a cover letter, they we are shutting off the process right from the start. This chapter looks at how to make them want to meet us – and get to know us better.

Just as with resumes, we create a number of pattern cover letters. Then we customize them for the particular industry, organization, ad, and person. Buyers can smell a generic cover letter a mile away, will toss it, and make a mental note not to open anything sent from us.

How we custom-make our cover letters begins with analyzing the help-wanted or the request for consulting services. What is it that they need or want? Usually that entails understanding the organization and how it communicates. If it is a buttoned-down one, the language will be indirect. We will have to ferret out what it is really saying. If it is out-there, it will spell out exactly what it wants and does not.

On the ad or the request we might have to read between the lines or contact an acquaintance about precisely the kind of fit we should present ourselves as. This is to be front-loaded, that is, in the second sentence and beyond we provide evidence that we are the best person. The first sentence demonstrates we know the organization or have a good sense of what it is about.

Here is an example:

Dear Mr. Smith:

Diamond Real Estate is, literally, the gem brandname here in the Baltimore area. For five years I have been helping real estate agencies reach the next level of revenue and profit through social media. For example, the team increased all Barnett's key numbers about 34 percent. From my research on Diamond, you seem poised to double just about every measurement.

The next paragraph goes on to briefly provide background information. We present the information which directly supports our application and responds to the organization's questions. Since we could be coming up against an age barrier, we do not want to discuss more than 10 years of experience. The focus will be on the most recent kind.

At this phase of the application procedure, we do not provide negatives or anything else such as a request for a telecommuting relationship three days a week which could knock us out of the box. The impression should be: We are the one you will choose.

The last paragraph is a call to action. If there is no specification against phone calls, then we tell the buyer we are calling next week. If the ad indicates no phone calls, we let the reader know how we can be reached.

If the search for the right candidate is a long one, we can follow up with breaking news such as a fresh accomplishment or congratulations about one of its accomplishments.

Is there room for gimmicks or hooks to get in the door? Of course. We can offer to let them try us out pro bono for a couple of days or draft a proposal about the company's public relations challenge. We can invite them to visit our shop, where they may get ideas. We can offer them an interview on our blog or podcast. There is even the possibility of live-blogging one of their open houses or instructional seminars. Our objective is to be noticed by them for our authentic interest in the business, our initiative, and our ability to execute.

If we get no or few responses then that is a red flag that our cover letters are not differentiating us from all the others applying. What do we do? Here are some recommendations:

Only reply to opportunities that we are interested in. That will motivate us to invest the effort in deconstructing the needs and then repackaging our credentials to fit. Otherwise we are just going through the motions and no one gets anything that way now.

Mirror the organizational culture. If we are applying to the Roman Catholic Diocese of Bridgeport, Connecticut, we will present ourselves as respectful, reserved, and wanting to make a difference. If we are applying to Google, we will present ourselves as innovative and ultra hard-working.

Ask for feedback. It is highly probable the employer or prospect will give it. They are sympathetic with our search for work. They may inform us that our cover letter is too long-winded, too bogged down in details of our background which do not matter, too stuck in the past, or too lacking in assertiveness.

Research selling fundamentals. We can sit in the bookstore or library a few hours a day finding out how people pitch effectively. When I wrote speeches for Kodak Chief Financial Officer Chris Steffen, he told me that he taught his team that the most important skill for an executive to have is the ability to sell ideas. Selling entails reaching out of ourselves and reaching into the world of the other person. It means forgetting our goal of getting the sale and being fully engaged with the prospect.

FAQs

Does a long long help-wanted indicate that we should reply in a similar detailed manner?

Here the principle of mirroring applies. We want to mirror the DNA or ethos of the organization. If that is very comprehensive and explicit, then that is how we respond. If that is not our comfort zone, then do not apply. We will be miserable even if we are hired. There are so many diverse workplace settings, we should all be able to find exactly the right organizational culture for us.

Are we wasting our time applying to youth-culture organizations like Google?

Not if we are youthful in our attitude, have done similar work, and have the track record to show. At go-go Apple, Steve Jobs is no spring chicken. No one is pushing him out.

Here is a general principle: All pitches for work, full time, part time, contingent, are Hail Mary Passes. It does not hurt to try.

Should we have cover letters professionally drafted?

There are those of us not talented with selling ourselves on paper. We might find it useful to contact someone or some vendor which knows the industry or profession to draft us pattern cover letters. The best way to find this help is to ask around for recommendations.

Sometimes we feel that we cannot send out yet one more cover letter? What do we do?

The Sabbath is a day of rest. We need to create our own versions of the Sabbath by taking a few hours off from a job or new-business search to regroup. A good night's sleep is also restorative. Research shows that we resolve emotional and professional problems through our dreams.

Another way to prevent being fried is to reflect on how much we are learning from this process. Then we might ask ourselves and those in our circle: How can we monetize this knowledge base? Perhaps we can start up a business creating cover letters.

What about the hidden marketplace? Opportunities not advertised?

Of course that still exists and is still the best source of work. We find a hook for contacting Joe Smith, the head of marketing at Corporation X.

Another way is to be visible ourselves so that they contact us, without our having to apply to them for work. How we are visible is through publishing books, articles and opinion-editorials in mainstream media, publishing on the web, delivering keynote speeches, serving in leadership positions in trade associations, and participating in controversy that we can manage.

Practice makes perfect? Or does it? Is there a learning curve with cover letters?

Usually yes, especially if we have been out of the job market for a while. We begin with our best shot. Very quickly, we will likely find out that our best shot does not get us a response. Then we invest more energy and imagination. We experiment with different approaches in cover letters. What does work will work quickly. We do more of that. We continue to do that until it stops working. The marketplace can change on a dime as to what tone and content it wants to see from those applying for work.

WHAT WE THINK WE KNOW:

- ❖ Cover letters are a type of dramatic performance. We are the actors. Employers and prospects are the audience. If we cannot get their attention immediately, they will ignore us.

- ❖ Through this introduction, we are inviting readers to take the next steps in the process, that is, look at our resume and any attachments, seek more information about us, and call us in for a personal interview.

- ❖ The more we invest in doing superb cover letters, the better results we will get. Usually, in this situation, sweat equity pays off.

CHAPTER 9

Interviews Are Two-Way Street

Those of us over-50 know from horrible job and client fits that interviews are a two-way street. They serve for us to size "them" us just as they are sizing us up. Once we have down cold the realities of the new economy and how to put ourselves out there effectively, we can afford to reject "them" if we do not want to work with them.

For those of us who can sell ourselves, there are plenty of opportunities out there. That means one thing: We can and should respond to that invitation to "get to know more about you" with the same wariness that they are applying to us.

The interview might be by email, phone, or in-person. From our point of view, it exists so that we can present ourselves as the best professional for that job or assignment, along with determining if it will cause us more agita than profit. From their point of view, it exists so that they can determine if we can do the job or assignment better than others and if we will present more problems that value.

In a sense this is the ultimate poker game. Both sides pretend this is a neutral encounter. Both sides are usually doing their best to conceal emotions and details about everything from the real job or assignment description to the range of compensation.

Both sides usually flatter themselves that they are brilliant players. Most are not, at least not to those of us over-50. We have down by now the various types we could be dealing with. That in itself helps us respond to type rather than to react to what often appears to be simple bad acting. The most common example is the human resources representative who wants to know the real Joe or Jane. Of course, we have no intention of bringing out the real Joe or Jane. We have every intention of bringing to life the best fit for the job or assignment.

The types we encounter when we search for work usually fall into two categories. The first is the charmers who are convinced that by delivering a bear hug they will seduce us into allowing them to pick our brain, divulge our negatives, and become way too relaxed.

The classic pattern is to praise us way too generously, take us out to a fancy meal, introduce us to the BigFoots as if we are already a member of the team, and then send some hardball questions our way and some pointed criticism, which is expected to throw us off balance. However, nothing will throw us off balance since we are familiar with the pattern. If we want the opportunity, we go along. This could be known as the Very Good Cop routine.

The second is the Very Bad Cop routine. The interviewers are difficult, but in a variety of diverse ways. In 2005, Robert M. Shapiro and Mark A. Jankowski wrote a book on just this subject. They are experts in dealing, including negotiating, with the Bad Cop kind. That book is "Bullies, Tyrants & Impossible People: How to Beat

Them Without Joining Them."

According to Shapiro and Jankowski, there are three types of difficult people. They are:

- √ The Situationally Difficult. They behave in an adversarial, abusive and/or angry manner because of the situation or the context. They may be the chief executive officer and the company is going down the tubes. They are scared and realize that this hire involves high stakes. Or they may be the Vice President of Marketing who has just been told he is finished at the company. He has to conduct this interview any way.

- √ The Strategically Difficult. They are convinced that bad behavior serves them and the company well. Count on them to feign anger. When I wrote for Lee Iacocca at Chrysler he seemed to use rage to get things done more quickly.

- √ The Simply Difficult. They suffer from low Emotional Intelligence [EI]. In some organizations they can get away with it. Usually those organizations are those which pay well. No one will rock the boat on this one.

No matter what combination or permutation of the Bad Cop we encounter, we are in control. That is because we understand what we are dealing with. We maintain emotional balance and move the interview along with neutral questions such as, "When will the company be making a decision in this hiring."

There is another part to the Bad Cop routine. That part is for us to decide if we want to be in that kind of environment. The Strategically Difficult, I found out, can drain us. For almost a decade I had such as client. The whole organization was programmed to do business in that manner. Finally, although it meant surrendering a hefty annual retainer fee, I opted out. After I hunted down replacement accounts, my only regret was not exiting after a year. Does lack of confidence make us stay on too long? My hunch is that it does. Greed might play a part too. We only have to earn enough to pay our bills. That is a lesson I am learning.

Whether Good or Bad Cop, the interview involves questions that we have to practice answering *before* they are asked. That is exactly why we are encouraged to grab hold of all the interviewing experience we can. We both become aware of the common concerns and gain experience answering them.

What are some of those concerns? Well, if we are engaging in a transition, that presents a red flag to organizations. That might be a switch from law to public relations or a migration from self-employment to full-time work for one employer.

No matter how well we provide answers, some organizations will not be satisfied that we can handle the change. That happened to me when interviewing with an insurance company. After the third set of interviews in which the same issue of my self-employment was raised, I told them I had secured another full-time position and was no longer available.

My mentor told me that I should have simply thanked them during the second interview for inviting me, packed up my Coach attaché case and left since I perceived they were stuck on one issue which has no relation to my skills to do the job. That experience was draining, with no payoff. We protect ourselves from those ordeals. Do not go. Do not continue in the process. Maybe we can blog about it. Maybe we can alert the Chief Executive

Officer how company time is being wasted in such a non-productive manner.

On the other hand, there will be organizations which we can convince that we are worth betting on. Interestingly, that happened to me, again self-employed, with another insurance company. They hired me, gave me a beginning bonus, and I learned a lot.

How we shape our answers usually comes from how we observe they are received. Based on those observations we may alter our tone, pacing, word choice, level of detail, admission of an error of judgment, and the laundry list of lessons learned.

We should not expect to get that perfect the first few times. Most of this is not intuitive but is derived from experience with how organizations operate and assess job and vendor applicants. As the cliché goes: Learn and eventually earn.

Given the intensity of competition, we will receive more rejections than offers. That means that we are probably closer to a Yes. It takes time to get the hang of acquiring the edge in presenting ourselves.

When I have been surprised at receiving a No, I have asked the interviewer for candid feedback. That approach has yielded a gold mine of insight. For example, when turned down for a full-time position at Boundless Playgrounds in Bloomfield, Connecticut, I requested input. The Executive Director took me to lunch and brought my first client. She said that I would do better as an entrepreneur and closer to Manhattan. I followed her advice.

There is no such entity as "losing out" on a job or assignment. We gained the interviewing experience as well as more in-depth knowledge of a kind of organization. The new economy is all about learning.

FAQs

On every interview we have been on the "they" were not satisfied with my answer for wanting a full-time position after being self-employed for five years. What are my options.

There are a number of options. One is to stay self-employed and to add to that temporary assignments and part-time work. Both of those are easier for an entrepreneur to obtain.

Another is change the story. The one we are presenting is not effective. Try others.

A third option is to apply for full-time jobs in organizations which put great value on entrepreneurial mindsets and track records. They are the most likely to let us in.

In an interview age came up. That is illegal. What should I do?

If age came up, maybe that is not the place to work. Obviously those in the interview loop are ham-handed about such issues. Real amateur hour. I accepted a full-time job with one of those. The man who was to be my first-line manager mentioned my age. I wanted the job too much. Mistake. My instincts were right. That manager was amateur hour. I left after a few months.

As we all know, introducing age is against the law. If there is evidence that issue was raised, then the matter can be reported to the EEOC, which has been very aggressive.

If harm has been done as a result of this, then a lawsuit might be considered. Most attorneys provide complimentary consultations. There is also the option to let it go. I have always let it go.

Do I have to grow a tougher skin? When the interviewers treat me badly I feel my dignity compromised.

If you want the opportunity you will practice responses to that kind of interviewing technique. In about 98% of cases, it is a tactic, nothing personal.

Practicing how to manage that tactic will insulate you from feeling less-than. It is a game. To play you must be totally prepared on your end how to push-back without losing control over the situation. In fact, the interviewers might be testing us out on how we field those kind of questions.

There are some of us who by time we reach over-50 choose not to enter organizations which operate via abuse, fear, and bullying. On the other hand there are those of us who will ignore all that in order to have access to the big money or the prestigious brandname.

There are no right answers on this. We have to choose our poison.

I interview poorly. What should I do?

No one interviews poorly. I reframe that with stating that some of us apply to organizations which we cannot navigate. I do not have an edge on my presentation of self when I am at over-the-top prestigious brandnames.

◄ OVER-50: HOW WE KEEP WORKING

You might examine where you are looking for work.

To improve interviewing skills watch the more serious talk shows such as those on Sunday morning. Observe how the guests and panel members handle themselves. There is also Alicia on "The Good Wife." She manages everything from confrontation to flirtation well. Note how tellers in banks, waitresses, and our investment advisors present themselves to their advantage.

After collecting our data, then we can ask a trusted friend to role play with us. There is also the option, if we are hunting big game, to hire a professional presentation coach.

When rejected for a job or assignment, should I keep in touch?

That would be shrewd if you have a hunch that you would be a good fit for another opportunity. In fact, in applying for assignments I have come to indicate that if I am not the best candidate for that assignment I would appreciate if they would consider me for another one. Over time, we can keep following up with notifying them of our fresh accomplishments.

Is it possible to come on too strong with personality?

Interviews are to find out if both parties can work together. They are not about getting to know us or about making friends. This is not dating. It is not campaigning for political office.

These days I would err on doing less personality than more.

INTERVIEWS ARE TWO-WAY STREET

WHAT WE THINK WE KNOW:

- ❖ Interviews are a two-way street. We are checking them out just like they are checking us out.

- ❖ If we are able to identify the types of roles interviewers take on, we can control that process. We will not react to seeming friendliness or abuse.

- ❖ Unless we are applying for a sales position, it is wise to hold the personality.

CHAPTER 10

Our Unique Power Strategies

Power is a must if we want to keep working. That is because power is the ability to get things done. That is how Washington D.C. journalist Hedrick Smith put it in his late 1980s classic on the subject "The Power Game." And what we want to get done is getting the kinds of jobs and assignments which we can leverage to get more jobs and assignments. Not all work is created equal.

Power is what separates players from the hand-wringing employee and angst-ridden entrepreneur. The ones with the power are the ones who define the rules of the game, change what is not giving us the edge, and flamboyantly disregard those that are sacred if controversy is going to serve us well.

The concept of power in professional life used to be taboo. In the late 1980s, my former client Bob Dilenschneider published a book on the subject which made him instantly a brandname in his field of public relations. That is because no Establishment type with the influence of Dilenschneider had brought up the subject in public. At the time he was the Chief Executive Officer of global public relations firm Hill & Knowlton.

◂ OVER-50: HOW WE KEEP WORKING

After he brought power out of the closet, mentors began to school us in how to acquire it, re-gain it when lost, and grow our empires, small and large. Women like myself were encouraged to learn how to do this, only in different ways than males did. For example, often, at least back in those days, we might be less direct and operate through consensus rather than attempting to seize power.

Now, of course, if we are not acquainted with power tools we are discounted as naïve, boy/girl scouts, capitalist virgins, and those who can be walked over. When over-50, we are expected to be knowledgeable about all power games and masters of several.

The fundamentals of power go like this:

√ Our primary goal is the advancement and protection of number-one, that is, ourselves. In this marketplace that includes learning as much as we can. When he delivered his now-famous Stanford University commencement speech, Steve Jobs talked about what he had learned in his life and how that came in handy. The professional in a public relations agency who knows social media has more power than those who do not. We will use that power to get what we need in terms of resources and what we want in terms of compensation or perks. If we do not use it we are fools. Power is a use it or lose in entity.

√ Power has many forms but all require an understanding of human nature. A hick from no where, Lyndon Johnson rose to the top because he could speedread human beings. He found out what they needed and wanted and gave that to them. We can enhance our ability to understand others by pouring into fiction. Management advisor Tom Peters

OUR UNIQUE POWER STRATEGIES

notes that fiction teaches him more than studying management texts.

√ Power dynamics mean rewarding allies, ignoring those who do not help us, and punishing those who attempt to harm us. Often this takes the form of revenge served cold, with a side of the exact right timing. Elizabeth Edwards, who seems to be a passive-aggressive power player, is allowing negative news to be released about John Edwards as he heads toward bottom. However, administering swift "justice" can also deliver a message that resonates.

√ We are open enough to be read for integrity but circumspect enough to remain mysterious. Unknowns, whether among other organizational members or Wall Street, inspire fear. Fear generates cooperation.

√ Our presence is always there, even when we are not. Presence is put together with many small actions and non-actions. The high-paid consultants at McKinsey Inc. create this through everything from the décor of the office, to their university background, to how they enter a room. Analyze how the big players create presence. An interesting case study of this can be done in the Park Avenue-based office of The Dilenschneider Group. Founder Bob Dilenschneider leases a half floor in that prestigious location. He travels by limo. He dines in restaurants where he will be seen and see others. In order to reach him at his office, we have to go through multiple receptionists. *This is presence.*

√ When we lose, we stoically embrace the development, learn from it, and come back stronger. Most leaders had lost before they made their big gains in title, status, and accomplishments. Hillary Clinton blew health-care reform early in her husband's first term in the White House. She laid low after that, making decisive moves after Bill Clinton finished his second term

√   We have third parties promote us. This could be as simple as our allies attending a trade association meeting and speaking well of our research. Simultaneously, we are impervious to praise. Those doing the gushing are not allies. They should be closely watched or dispatched to the wilderness.

There are an infinite number of ways to power. How we go about this depends primarily on our strengths and background. Regarding the latter, Rupert Murdoch, who at one time had been a formidable media tycoon in the print era, studied at Oxford when game theory was the rage. A useful read on the subject is the 2007 brief book "Game Theory: A Very Short Introduction" by Ken Binmore. Those proficient in the tenets of this erudite subject can out-fox the competition and enemies much of the time.

Some who want to improve their power game read about those who went for big stakes and did well. For instance, German history author Giles MacDonogh analyzes Adolf Hitler's key moves in the year 1938. Giles recently published a book with that title. It demonstrates that Hitler got the support and resources he needed not simply through the force of his personality or charisma and the devastated condition of Germany. He would use internal crises in his administration as an excuse for a high-profile reorganization. When that was taking place, he would make the stealth changes he needed to put in place.

OUR UNIQUE POWER STRATEGIES

Here are some of the most effective power tools:

- √ Likeability. It is easier to work with those we like. Bill Clinton is a very likable rascal. Hillary Clinton would have gone much further in her own career if she could play the likeability card.

- √ Ability to be an obstacle or an obstructionist. This is sometimes called "Porcupine Power." Those with swing votes in the U.S. Senate can get just about anything they want. Players find positions where they can be in charge of resources and granting favors. The typical job for stealth power is that of administrative assistant in a political office or the trusted secretary for a business executive.

- √ The reputation for having clout. It does not have to be true. Some attempt to create this image with the symbols of power such as being photographed with leaders.

- √ Unique expertise. The smart player protects this and only doles out what is directly reimbursed. Some public relations boutiques still have the mantra: Do not ever educate the client or make what we do seem easy. However, the risk here is that the unique expertise becomes not so unique or out of date.

- √ Confidence. This quality is rare among professionals. When they spot it in others they defer to it. Too much confidence, however, can lead to arrogance and that is a prerequisite to career collapse.

- √ Willingness to listen. When we allow people to be taken seriously we create loyalists. Caroline Kennedy did not do too well when she went on her listening tour in the key political area of Upstate New York. She never became a candidate for the U.S. Senate.

√ Visibility. We are always there. In Connecticut, the Attorney General Richard Blumenthal does not miss any opportunity to intervene. He just won the battle to keep well-paid union jobs at Pratt & Whitney in Connecticut. In this media age, the danger of overexposure is less than underexposure.

√ Attractiveness. Remember the face that launched a 1000 ships. John Edwards might not have gotten as far as he did in politics had it not been for his good looks. Eleanor Roosevelt probably would have gone further in her career had she addressed her appearance.

√ Energy. The new economy runs on a speeded-up metabolism. Politico.com did in Establishment the WASHINGTON POST because the journalists operated on steroids. If the Obama dog was out on the White House lawn, they caught that development and posted in immediately. Psychologist John F. Gartner contends in his 2005 book "The Hypomanic Edge," that the U.S. became the dominant economy because it was settled by extreme-energy misfits.

√ Timing. When Apple was in trouble, it rehired Steve Jobs. When the nation was tired of the Bill and Hillary show it voted in the George and Laura show. It seems to already be tired of the Barack and Michelle show. The ability to read emerging trends can lead to power.

√ Success. That is why what a leader does in the first 100

days is so important. The aura surrounding Apple is from its string of successes. If the iPad stumbles, Apple takes on a new vulnerability.

There are also an infinite ways to not get power and to lose it. Here are just some:

- √ Neediness. Those around us will give us what we need, such as praise or attention, then eat our power lunch.

- √ Inability to change. The good people flee. Everyone in the know notices this. Power evaporates.

- √ Blaming. Savvy from all the information in the media, others understand this as a defensive move. They find a better bunch to support. Had Massachusetts Democrats not played the blame game after they lost the election to GOP Scott Brown, they would have awakened support from diverse new people. No one respects a cry baby.

- √ Failure to take decisive action in a timely fashion. Members of the mob have this fundamental down cold.

In youth, applying power dynamics gives us a competitive advantage. Over-50, they are part of our job description or service contract with a client. Power draws what we want to us. The lack of power creates vacuums. Those holes will be filled efficiently by those who know power and that it is a use-it-or-lose-it phenomenon.

◄ OVER-50: HOW WE KEEP WORKING

WHAT WE THINK WE KNOW:

- ❖ The workplace knows all about power. If we do not we will be sidelined as a capitalist virgin.

- ❖ Power is a use it or lose it tool. When we do not use it we lose it, not just the chance to gain an advantage.

- ❖ There are an infinite number of ways to acquire, re-gain, and add to power. Those depend on our strengths and background.

CHAPTER 11

Adversity Is Good

We are probably the walking wounded, at least professionally. And that is an advantage.

Some smart companies always knew the utility of suffering to professional performance. For example, at the end of the 1980s, I was ghostwriting a chapter for a book on executive development. GE allowed us an interview about its in-house management training program. It only admitted high-potential employees after they had suffered career disappointments and setbacks. It was only then, asserted the company, that those high-potential employees were willing to listen and apply what they were learning. Before that it was a safe bet that they were closed systems.

Fortunately, there are plenty of disappointments and setbacks to go around. In fact, they are the new normal. More does not happen than does happen. And just about everything takes longer than we anticipated. Those of us who can adjust to this new normal are the 21st-century winners in the workforce. We are better equipped to manage the next round of professional obstacles.

In fact, many of us wind up "better off than we were." That does not necessarily mean earning more money or having more status or fame or recognition. It could simply mean the inner strength of a survivor. That is not to be discounted in an economy which will continue to sneak up and surprise us. But being "better off" could also mean more satisfaction from the work we do, an increased ability to take risks, and reduced fear about what superiors might say.

When we are over-50, the lion's share of us will wind up in different space. It is unlikely we will get another traditional job or even stay in the same field of specialization. Once we accept that, the migration to what is next tends to proceed without the usual agita. The best payoff is that we usually do find that we can do work —and *like it* — that we never ever considered trying.

At age 60, I proved myself a giant on the web. I *liked it* so much that I turned down opportunities in my former field of executive communications. This was me, one-time techno phobic

A former IT employee at a multi-national company discovered his passion for transportation. He leveraged old skills and experience and new ones he learned in courses online to a job in city government. That is a whole new career for him.

An administrative cog in the book publishing industry found out she could put together online video trailers. Now she owns an enterprise which specializes in that.

At first, of course, none of us welcomed the career disruptions that had been thrust upon us. But we did not resist, at least not totally. We allowed what was to be next to happen.

And then there are those, years after a layoff or the tanking of a business, who are still in that same space. They might be bottom-fishing or living off credit cards hoping "things will turn around." They have no intention of considering other ways of making a living. By now, their spouses have left them or ignore them. Their children tiptoe on eggshells around them. They look aged beyond their years.

Why can some move on after adversity and wind up better off and some stay stuck?

Both Harvard Law School professor Rosabeth Kanter ["Confidence"] and management consultant Jim Collins ["How The Mighty Fall"] observe there is a point of no return. If we allow a changing situation to deteriorate to that point, individuals as well as organizations cannot pull out. There are bankruptcies, suicides, and delusion states of denial.

That means that we have to move toward stability and then forward while we still have resources, options about what to try out, optimism, support from others, and hope. Here are some tactics to prevent a bad time from turning into a complete downward trajectory which cannot be halted.

- √ Get it that there is a fine line between an event we did not wish for and one that throws us into chaos. Once in chaos, we might fall victim to both the external and internal turbulence. We cannot battle on both fronts. We have to remain calm to navigate the volatility outside.

- √ Take immediate steps to conserve cash. Often those who were "forced" to do this later say they are relieved to have fewer weighty fixed costs.

- ✓ Find work, any kind. It does not matter that we have tons of severance or are eligible for unemployment. Paid work restores our confidence in our ability to survive. Around our schedule of work hours we can contemplate what is next.

- ✓ Create a cover story. Stick with it. Despite this being the end of the era of Oprah, some assume they have to confide *everything*. We owe no one but our family any explanation, any details, any expression of innermost feelings. A cover story which satisfies others is short with enough detail to make them glaze over. For example, "Right now, I'm dealing with too much choice. X contacted me about full-time work, Y wants consulting services, and me, I still have the dream of running my business." We do not have to discuss our interim jobs.

- ✓ Invest ourselves in approaching this challenge so we can learn from it. That goal will keep us focused on getting something out of the experience as well as continuing to be positive. Adversity is the best teacher. It is a crime to waste those lessons being handed to us.

- ✓ Explore other ways to make a living. If we are typical we earned our bread in a professional bunker. Our networks, values, and skills were all tied to one field. We find out how others who are not so different from us make a living. We candidly ask is we could also start out in their fields. For example, the unemployed journalist or editor might interview the public relations representative or lobbyist who lives in the neighborhood. The laid-off corporate manager takes out the manager of Petco to lunch. Could she run a whole store? After all, she understands systems, motivating people, preventing theft, and doing course correction.

√ We allow our loved ones, support personnel such as therapists and coaches, and helpers in the community such as ministers to hold us afloat.

Some of us wonder if we will ever heal from that time of sudden and seeming sustained uncertainty? Of course, we will. And we will do it several times in our long lives. Just look around us. There probably is not any human being over-50 who has not been sucked up in a tornado of change. If it is not the way of making a living, it is a divorce, the drug problem of a child, a neighborhood which has become crime-ridden, cancer, death of a parent, a house under-water which causes us to think the unthinkable which is walk away from the mortgage.

Those who create new value from this experience are the ones who do not position it as crisis. It is a change of circumstance to be embraced, addressed, and its lessons never forgotten.

FAQs

Does everyone feel shame after being laid off? Me? I am most sheepish about not seeing it coming.

Perhaps it is not shame that we are feeling as much as loss, which is a strong emotion. In America, what we do to make our living is central to our identity as well as our sense of belonging, and status. When we lose that bundle, we lose a lot. We have to permit ourselves to mourn.

Shame? It is not like we have been nailed for criminal activity. During this ordeal, and it is an ordeal, anyone who treats us as if we should be ashamed is not an ally.

Unless we could have prevented the Reduction-in-Force by "seeing it coming," that is irrelevant. What is relevant is resuming a way to make a living.

Adversity is harder to endure when just about the whole neighborhood has been laid off. We all were employed by the same manufacturer.

This is no time for banding together. Research and experience show that socializing and networking with the unemployed are counterproductive. We have to keep lines open with the working. If the neighborhood is engulfed in the dark night of the soul, we get out of it daily and conduct our search for what is next from the public library, career center at the university, official outplacement or, best of all, a part-time job we have at Starbucks.

Research on mirror neurons proves that we human beings influence each other cell by cell. Psychologist Daniel Goleman says the best investment we can make in our career is carefully choosing those we associate with. We are our networks. That is exactly why some contend we can speedread what a person or professional is all about by just looking at his or her inner circles. We bond with those at our same level of maturity of immaturity.

Why does it take hard times to learn what we need to?

Hard times are not the only teacher. We would not be where we have been had we not been able to also grow from success.

What is amazing about suffering is that all its brutal lessons tend to be noticed. At those critical times, we are not selective learners.

In addition, to relieve the pain we will probably do anything, including thinking and acting outside the box. THE NEW YORK TIMES covered unemployed architect John Morefield. He had been laid off twice. That led him to set up a booth at a farmers's market in Seattle. He put a sign on it: *Architecture 5-cents*. That is how he has picked up enough assignments to make a good living again.

Does "it" – that is, the upheaval – ever seem smooth sailing?

Most of us come to know the drill. We take the right steps, timed right. Things fall into place more quickly. So, it seems less traumatic to absorb the blow, take emergency action, and then try out tactics to re-join the workforce.

WHAT WE THINK WE KNOW:

- ❖ The dark nights of the soul which we are moving through have likely enhanced every part of our professional lives.

- ❖ In a downward trajectory, it has been shown to be a point of no return. We need to pull out of career setback before we reach that.

- ❖ Unemployment can be contagious. That is not where we should be socializing or networking.

CHAPTER **12**

Thinking the Unthinkable: Going blue collar

Recently Schneider National Inc. announced that it was hiring 2500 new drivers. That was to accommodate the growing freight base of this $3.7 billion provider of trucking, logistics, and intermodal services. The manpower would be recruited in the West, Southwest, Midwest, Southeast, and Northeast.

How many unemployed, underemployed or unhappily employed white collar employees paid attention to this notice? Likely very few. We over-50 were conditioned from the get-go to get the education to become white collar. This is one of those deep values that we might not even be aware of. The problem is that it may not be functional any more.

Back in those days the economy was moving to a knowledge one. The need was for educated manpower who could fill the slots in what became known as Corporate America. Success was programmed as landing a position in GM, U.S. Steel, or Colgate-Palmolive. But it was also okay to train to join a profession such as law, medicine, or advertising. Just keep that collar white. The more prestige the slot had, the better.

Currently, the knowledge economy has given way to what many like Daniel Pink and Richard Florida call the Right Brain or Creative Economy. Education is not so necessary. What counts more is the ability to see emerging trends and shape a product or service to align with it. Steve Jobs and Bill Gates are both college dropouts. The Internet allows any of us to obtain exactly what we need in terms of education and training without a degree. And, maybe sooner than later "degrees" will become anachronisms. Certification for a job or assignment might take a different form.

Also, it is predicted that by 2020, the university as we have known it, will disappear. Higher education will be delivered online for relative peanuts. That great divide between the educated and uneducated will be forever blurred. The plumber wants to learn Shakespeare? He or she will take a course on the web, compose a type of history drama with four fellow students in four different nations, and meet on Saturdays with the professor by phone.

There is more. Those once plentiful knowledge-worker white collar positions keep shrinking. Technology and outsourcing will continue to reduce their number. Actually right now, reports THE WALL STREET JOURNAL, about 23% of us — almost a fourth — are already freelancers or no collar workers. We earn our living just-in-time, when clients and customers need us. Most of us are stationed in offices at home, wearing no collar. If we perform tasks onsite at the client's headquarters, we are likely invisible.

So, why not drive a truck for a while or for the longer term? We would probably make more than most freelancers in the writing field. More importantly, we would have an insider view on a type of work, a company, and an industry. If we are unemployed or underemployed lawyers we might be able to leverage that insight into a position with a federal regulatory agency, a trucking trade association, a union, or even the company itself.

In 2003, I migrated from being an almost bankrupt white collar communications boutique owner to a blue collar contract loss prevention employee aka security guard. Very quickly, my energy, focus, and customer-service skills were noticed. First they offered me the supervisor's job. I turned it down because the money was not worth the enormous responsibility, both in terms of the customers and the workforce.

Later I submitted a marketing plan. The higher-ups recommended me for a marketing position in headquarters. After I did my due diligence on the company I discovered it was ripe for a hostile take-over. That is exactly what happened. The payoff is what I learned about myself and the world of work. That included:

- √ In most workplaces I would be perceived as an excellent worker. That meant, despite my age then which was 58, I had a shot at a promotion. Therefore, my success was *not in the past and not tied to one profession or line of work*. If I continued to keep my eyes open I would spot many potential opportunities. Yes, there was a big world out there. I had missed all that when I was buried in one area of expertise, trying to hang on to my upper middle class lifestyle.

- √ Earning a living need not mean chronic worry and stress. Most of my co-workers showed up for the pay check with the added bonus of socializing and passing on gossip. No one, including me, brought work home. My energy was freed up enough to build what would be next.

- √ That supposed line between white and blue collars has

become fuzzy. There was simply working. Some of my co-workers did have college degrees or parts of them. What was valued by supervision was the ability to do that job in the way that was specified and getting along with everyone.

√ Networking is second nature among the working class. I received more help getting back on my feet from supervisors and co-workers than I had ever before. This confirms the research by sociologist Mark Granovetter that it is those weak links or those ties outside our typical networks which get us jobs. It is Joe who runs the newsstand who knows of all the openings in the office building or the bar tender who tips us off about a firing about to go down and therefore a breaking opportunity for us. Not only are they in the know. They view us differently than our usual professional contacts who tend to pigeon-hole us as to what we can and cannot do. When we venture outside our homogenous groupings we encounter more possibilities.

√ Nothing is forever. Instead of building seniority, we accumulate skills, knowledge and insight about how to get in and get ahead in diverse work environments.

An acquaintance had been in the installation department of a medical supplier. By time he had been forced out he had become weary of the dynamics of organizational life. He studied for his commercial driver's license and is now making almost as much working for a limo company as an independent contractor.

A writer I had hired on a contract basis trained to be a dog groomer. She works at two different pet retail stores. Eventually she hopes to have her own mobile grooming business.

THINKING THE UNTHINKABLE: GOING BLUE COLLAR

After we take the plunge, no one who has seems to care about the nature of the collar. Not anymore. It is too much of a relief to be bringing home money and not having earning a living take too much out of us. Remember on "Without a Trace," FBI agent Jack Malone was in mandatory therapy. His issue was why he allowed the job to cost him so much. Poor Malone, he was one of those true walking wounded unable to manage the "terrorists within."

It is also likely that the working class will assume white collar jobs. My hairdresser became first a demonstrator, then a sales representative for a color company. Her boss clued her in about getting down cold the corporate language and then what to say on sales calls to close. Aside from that, there was no adjustment nervous breakdown.

A clerk in a big box rose to manage a territory. She did not have to unlearn those Fortune 100 ways of dressing and talking. Everyone, ranging from the higher-ups to the subordinates, loves her. She is real.

A retired factory worker started out as a homecare aide. Eventually she was promoted to an administrative position. Instinctually she got the hang of how to be more formal.

The media describe us "falling from the middle class." For those who are going through economic and social gyrations the results may be, ironically, to land on more solid ground. Maintaining a middle class lifestyle is expensive and emotionally stressful. Just aiming to make the best living we can might be a whole lot easier.

So, yes, ask that admissions director at the trade school what kind of training and at what cost it would be to become an EMT, electrician, roofer, plumber, or massage therapist. All collars seem to be the same when we are paying our bills on time, paying off credit card bills, and enjoying parts of life not related to work.

That so-called "fall from grace" might be waking up to common sense. Moreover, where we first land does not mean that is where we will stay. In her 2001 book "Nickel and Dimed," Barbara Ehrenreich describes low-paying slots in the economy in which few seem to understand how to improve their earning ability. That world is dark. Ours does not have to be. If we had initiative and creativity before, we can marshal it again. And, who knows, we might establish a pilot program to train those earning minimum wage how to "get ahead."

WHAT WE THINK WE KNOW:

- ❖ Those firewalls between white, blue, pink, and no collars are being removed. They tended to be 20th-century post-WW II artificial structures.

- ❖ Higher education will be less of the Great Divide. The web will make more accessible and lower cost what people want or need to learn. Certification for jobs and assignments might be unbundled from academic degrees.

- ❖ Being between collars might show us that earning a living need not be so stressful.

- ❖ Where we land after a career reversal does not mean where we will remain.

CHAPTER **13**

Being a Late Bloomer

Now 94, Carmen Herrera sold her first painting at 89. Her work now is exhibited at the Museum of Modern Art, the Hirshhorn Museum and the Tate Modern.

Frank Lloyd Wright started on Fallingwater after age 65.

Henrik Ibsen wrote the play "Hedda Gabler" when he was past 60.

I published my first work of fiction, the novel "The Fat Guy From Greenwich," at age 64.

Researchers in all disciplines tell us that the ability to blossom does not stop at a certain age. For example, psychiatrist Julian Lieb documents that creativity does not lessen with age. It does not have to skip a beat. If it declines, it could be because we have become lazy, depressed, or physically ill.

Economics expert David Galenson goes further. In his study of genius he found that some manifestations of it do not come together until late in life. In his book "Old Masters and Young Geniuses,"

Galenson posits a theory. There are those such as Mozart whose talent bursts out in such a way that they are recognized early in life. Then there are others who keep experimenting with a variety of styles or approaches. Finally, they can put all that together in a way that is hailed "genius." Sometimes this involves having the confidence to stop imitating others and take a leap into innovation. When I called a halt to mirroring the style of Tom Wolfe, I began to find my own voice. That was at age 60.

Given that we are living longer, there is more opportunity for us to let ourselves become all we can be. In Manhattan, Jane Gilenan is 111. She worked full-time until she was in her early 80s. Currently, there are more than 70 people around the world who are 110 or older [Source: Gerontology Research Group.]

Clint Eastwood came into his own with "The Unforgiven," after he had been around seemingly forever. Then he came up with "Million Dollar Baby." He is still surprising us.

Dave Letterman continues to develop. No one in that late-night category can come near him in talent and performance.

There is no telling what new and fresh will come from Oprah Winfrey once she departs her niche of the talk show.

What separates those who blossom from those who do not? Often adversity plays a role. After the dark night of the soul, we tend to not seek safety so much. In fact, we realize how fragile a state that is. We find a wild source of courage and innovation within us.

It was mothers who had lost their children who had founded that game-changer Mothers Against Drunk Drivers. It made being drunk not funny — and illegal behind the wheel of a car.

BEING A LATE BLOOMER

Early rejection by white-shoe law firms might have helped shaped the rebel in Alan Dershowitz. He channeled that into approaching criminal trials in ways that won acquittals.

The three defense teams who lost the Rhode Island lead paint trial came back to have it tossed by the state's Supreme Court. No one expected that.

It is well-known that tough childhoods tend to produce the big success stories in work. The creator of "Peanuts" Charles Schulz refused to seek psychotherapy. He feared, perhaps rightly so, that such "help" would destroy his talent.

Another factor could be the willingness to sacrifice. Succeeding in a breakthrough manner does not happen by living the conventional middle-class lifestyle. There is something to the writers and artists who work at their craft in dire straits. Think about those at the Chelsea Hotel in Manhattan. Some like Patti Smith became famous and rich. Steve Jobs could be the patron saint of eccentrics. Of course, lack of material comforts and "Honey, I'm home" do not guarantee that we will blossom. However the odds are we will not if we are boxed into the traditional demands a traditional lifestyle puts on people.

A third factor is being open to the world, just as it is. Andy Warhol took in that pop culture was framing how the masses saw cans of soup and former first ladies. He could have judged and been critical. Instead he observed and made silk screens of what he saw.

Blossoming is not restricted to art, inventions, or schools of thought. It could be simply mastering our small part of the work universe. We come to be saluted in our organization for how we can orchestrate a turnaround or in our own solo business for how we can train dogs. One day we are average. Then we become a master, sought after by employers and clients.

How can we increase the odds that we will give genius a shot? Here are some suggestions:

- √ Ditch the confidence in experts, conventional wisdom, and what others have said are our strengths and weaknesses. We deserve to check everything out for ourselves. We may find, Malcolm Gladwell did and does, that certain peculiar patterns seem to operate and no one has described them and where they can be applied. Or we may discover a unique way of communicating using digital technology. We may create a stupid pet trick that goes viral on YouTube.

- √ Channel fewer resources into making our current work or career a homerun. We need to make a living. But the pursuit of outstanding achievement might be suppressing our genius. Excellence in the workplace may be overrated.

- √ Do not care, at least not so much. The Buddhists call it not being attached. The Christians call it wearing life like a loose garment. The detached stumble upon things.

- √ Lend an ear to emerging schools of thinking, art, process management, and education. Bits and pieces of that might fall into place for our own projects.

We can blossom more than once. Look at the careers of Marlon Brando, Edie Falco, Jamie Dimon, Ana Marie Cox, and Buddy Cianci. The first time is just the hardest.

WHAT WE THINK WE KNOW:

- ❖ There is a category of genius known as Late Bloomers.

- ❖ Conventional mindsets and lifestyles can prevent us from being all we can bet.

- ❖ We can blossom many times.

Conclusion

We are the front lines of one of the biggest experiments in the history of mankind: Wanting to work over-50. That means we will be creating new strategies and tactics to stay in the workforce. Those, in turn, will create new models, ranging from organizational policies to our legal system to lifestyles. And those models will be observed, deconstructed, written about, and judged. As we were in our young adulthood, we are again center-stage. Come watch us at The Revolution.

About the Author

Jane Genova helps those over-50 stay working. She is a coach and conducts workshops at organizations such as the New York Bar State Bar Association. Her publications on careers include "The Critical 14 Years of Your Professional Life," "Geezer Guts: Earning a Buck At Any Age," and "Seeking Salvation on Park Avenue, K Street and Greenwich, CT." She operates two syndicated career sites http://careertransitions.typepad.com, http://over-50.typepad.com. Her communications background includes presentations and promotions http://janegenova.com. She resides in New Haven, Connecticut.